DRAGON'S WINE AND ANGEL'S BREAD

Dragon's Wine
AND
Angel's Bread

The Teaching of Evagrius Ponticus
on Anger and Meekness

GABRIEL BUNGE

translated from the German by
ANTHONY P. GYTHIEL

ST VLADIMIR'S SEMINARY PRESS
CRESTWOOD, NEW YORK
2009

Library of Congress Cataloging-in-Publication Data

Evagrius, Ponticus, 345?–399.
  [Drachenwein und Engelsbrot. English]
  Dragon's wine and angel's bread : the teaching of Evagrius Ponticus on anger and
meekness / Gabriel Bunge ; translated from the German by Anthony P. Gythiel.
      p. cm.
  Includes bibliographical references and index.
  ISBN 978-0-88141-337-3 (alk. paper)
    1. Anger—Religious aspects—Christianity—Early works to 1800. 2. Theology,
Doctrinal—History—Early church, ca. 30–600. I. Bunge, Gabriel, 1940–. II. Title.
  BR65.E923D7313 2009
  241'.3—dc22

                                                                2009032715

Translation copyright © 2009

ST VLADIMIR'S SEMINARY PRESS
575 Scarsdale Rd, Crestwood, NY 10707
1-800-204-2665
www.svspress.com

Cover image: *Stuttgarter Psalter*, St Denis, 9th cent.
Württembergische Landesbibliothek, Stuttgart, bibl. fol. 23.

A translation of Gabriel Bunge, *Drachenwein und Engelsbrot.*
Die Lehre des Evagrios Pontikos von Zorn und Sanftmut

ISBN 978-0-88141-337-3

PRINTED IN THE UNITED STATES OF AMERICA

"Thou shalt tread upon the lion and adder; the young lion and the dragon shalt thou trample under foot": [Christ] redeems us from the asp and the basilisk, which are opposed to *praktikē*, and he protects us from the lion and the dragon, which are opposed to contemplation. (*In Ps.* 91:13)

Table of Contents

Agressiveness—An Entirely Natural Matter?

From time immemorial, the world in which we live has been marked by violence: violence among persons, even violence against unborn life, violence also in international relations, and finally violence against nature and the environment on which our existence depends. Since Cain's killing of Abel, the law of violence has held sway.

Modern psychology has endeavored to interpret this omnipresent "aggressiveness," i.e., the desire to attack, as "natural" and even necessary. However, nothing has been improved by this. Well-meaning organizations like the United Nations certainly try to keep within bounds the general violence between peoples—sometimes even by using violence. Nonetheless, humanity's aggressiveness has not thereby diminished—quite the contrary. Rather, it would seem that the violence against men and things increases unceasingly, especially in civilized and "peace-loving" states. It is as if "the devil has been let loose."

And this is indeed so. "The whole world is in the power of the evil one,"[1] not just of an impersonal "evil," but in the power of a personal, absolute "Evil," Satan. Nowadays, many enlightened minds, having officially "taken leave from the devil," do not hear this gladly. It smacks too much of obscurantism and seems only to further the growing "culture of evil." A German proverb says, "One should not paint the devil on the wall." But the opposite is true! Evil in all its forms, and the Evil One himself, must be called by its name: only in this way is it found out.

---

[1] 1 John 5:19.

To be sure, Satan has nothing against one speaking of a "natural aggressiveness of man," for much can be concealed behind this. Since, according to modern understanding, this "aggressiveness" is "natural" and thereby in principle morally neutral, one must simply live with this. This is what most people then do, to the detriment of all—even in the Church. What is surprising is that to a certain extent, it has always been like this—even when the modern concept of "aggressiveness" did not exist and one spoke of "irascibility" (θυμικόν) as a power of the soul, while "anger" (θυμός) and "wrath" (ὀργή) counted as vices. The history of the Church, which was of course founded by him who said of himself that he is "meek and lowly in heart" and who taught us that one should learn precisely these qualities from him,[2] is filled with violence.

On this point, we are not even thinking of medieval events such as the Crusades or the burning of witches, which are often cited in this context. More surprising is the aggressiveness also of many clerics in their dealings with their peers, especially when the other is convicted or merely suspected of heresy. Even famous "church Fathers" had no problem allowing their unbridled aggressiveness to be expressed at least verbally. A prominent victim of this aggressiveness within the Church was a man who himself thought much on "anger": Evagrius Ponticus (ca. 345–99),[3] a student first of Basil the Great and Gregory of Nazianzus, and then later as a monk in the Egyptian desert, of Macarius the Great and his namesake from Alexandria. In Evagrius, one finds a finely honed teaching on anger worthy of reflection. Evagrius is also the great teacher of "prayer," of the mystical life, whom all later authors have copied, either directly or indirectly. But misguided aggressiveness, which only a few ever take into consideration, is the greatest enemy of the spiritual life in general and the deadly enemy of prayer in particular.

When the depraved demon has done all he can and still finds that his efforts to prevent the prayer of the virtuous man are unavailing,

---

[2]Matt 11:29.
[3]On Evagrius, see G. Bunge, *Evagrios Pontikos. Briefe aus der Wüste. Sophia*, vol. 24. Trier: Paulinus-Verlag, 1986 (Introduction A and B).

he will let up for a time. But again after a while he avenges himself on this man of prayer. For he will either enkindle the man's anger and thus dissipate that excellent state established in him by prayer, or else he chooses to outrage the spirit by provoking it to some unreasonable pleasure.[4]

*

My purpose is not to deal with the theme of "anger" in Evagrius either scientifically or exhaustively. It is more important, it seems to me, to elaborate on the spiritual insights that the Pontian monk had attained in order to make them useful for one's own spiritual life. For what good is it to speak in a well-informed manner and "with pleasure of the deeds of the Fathers," when one does not desire for oneself with the greatest effort to achieve such deeds?[5] *Mutatis mutandis*, that would be the same as with faith for the demons: it does not profit them in the least.[6]

*

Meanwhile, one would misunderstand Evagrius completely if one were satisfied with merely stigmatizing vice. Like evil in general, passion has no being in itself. It always presents itself only as a disease (also called πάθος [disease]) secondarily as a parasite on the soul and its powers, which are "healthy by nature" on account of their being created by God.[7] In short, vice is always only a perversion of a being that was created good. Thus, anger too is nothing other than a contranatural malfunctioning of one of the two irrational (and yet in themselves good[8]) powers of the soul: namely, the irascible power (θυμικόν). Its operation "according to nature," however, is nothing other than the virtue opposed to the vice.

A vice, then, cannot be understood or resisted effectively if one does not previously know the virtue that is its opposite. But the lat-

---

[4]*Or.* 47.
[5]*Eul.* 16.
[6]Cf. Jas 2:19.
[7]Cf. *KG* I.41; *Pr.* 56.
[8]Cf. *Pr.* 86.

ter can be known only to the extent that one practices it and makes it one's own. In the case of anger, this virtue is Christian love (ἀγάπη),[9] which manifests itself as forbearance, patience, and the like; but for Evagrius, above all as "meekness" (πραότης).

Meek love brings about exactly what contranatural anger hinders. While the latter disturbs contemplation since it "blinds" the intellect,[10] that "mother of knowledge"[11] turns the intellect into a "contemplative.[12] And while anger makes prayer impossible,[13] "prayer in 'spirit and in truth' becomes effective in perfect and spiritual love."[14] Much is at stake, then. Whoever allows himself to be ruled by anger fails to fulfill his own destiny as a creature. For the intellect was created precisely to "know,"[15] and prayer in which the knowledge of God reaches its apogee of development is "the activity which is appropriate to the dignity of the spirit; or better, it is appropriate for its nobler and adequate operation."[16] Therefore, whoever strives for "true prayer" and is angry or resentful must be out of his mind,[17] being as insane as the person who would want to see clearly and pokes out his eyes with an iron needle.[18]

What is at stake is our "dignity" as God's creatures gifted with reason (λόγος), who thanks to this ability are capable of having an immediate personal relationship with our Creator. For what would remain to man if he failed to attain this, his real destiny?

[9]*Ibid.* 38.
[10]*KG* IV.47; V.27.
[11]*Ep.* 27.2.
[12]*Ibid.* 27.4.
[13]*Or.* 27.
[14]*Ibid.* 77.
[15]*KG* I.50, 87, 89.
[16]*Or.* 84.
[17]*Ibid.* 65.
[18]*Ibid.* 64; *Gn.* 5.

CHAPTER I

The Evagrian Image of Man

In order to understand the prominent meaning Evagrius ascribes to anger—and even more so to its opposite, love or meekness—in the spiritual life, it is necessary above all to keep before one's eyes the image of man that he presumes in this. First, we shall content ourselves here with a general outline or sketch; particular aspects will be discussed later.

The foundations of the Evagrian image of man are of a biblical nature at the core, despite strong Greek philosophical wording at times. It is always a question of man, who is created in his "intellect" (νοῦς)—his personal core—"in the image of God"[1]: a quality he does not lose as a "fallen image"[2] or a sinner.[3] Nonetheless, this "old man, who is destroyed as a consequence of deceitful lusts,"[4] first of all requires a fundamental "renewal in the image of his Creator,"[5] making him a "new creation in Christ,"[6] before he becomes open to accepting God's grace. This "renewal" occurs in holy baptism,[7] and it is this "new man" who becomes a true "receiver of the knowledge of the Father" through the Son and the Spirit,[8] whose "true image" he really is.[9]

---

[1]Gen 1:27 (all citations LXX); *Scholia on the Psalms* (*In Ps.*) 38:6 δ et passim.
[2]*Gnostikos* (*Gn*) 50.
[3]*In Ps.* 118:113 ν.
[4]Eph 4:22.
[5]Col 3:10; *In Ps.* 77:34 ιδ et passim.
[6]2 Cor 5:17.
[7]*Letter on Faith* (*Ep. fid.*) 11.9 f.
[8]*Letter to Melania* (*Ep. Mel.*) 16.
[9]*Ep. Mel.* 19.

Every human being, with whom the discourse will deal subsequently, is also always the baptized one—"the one established as a new man created after God,"[10] even when his new being is always being threatened by a backsliding into its former depravity. That Evagrius in this context speaks almost exclusively about monks should not surprise us: his readers were mostly monks and nuns living in community or as anchorites. For Evagrius, the "monk" is simply the prototype of the "new man": what turns a "man" in this sense into a "monk" is that he first turns away from all actual sins. His intellect becomes a "monk" when it is free of all sins of thought, and "perceives the light of the Holy Trinity at the time of prayer."[11] The following oft-cited definition of a "monk" should also be understood as corresponding to this: "A monk is one who is separated from all and who is in harmony with all."[12]

Just as the one who withdraws into uninhabited regions is not for this reason already an "anchorite," but rather earns this name only when he "lives devoutly and justly in the world that is taking shape in his mind,"[13] so too does it not suffice simply to live "alone" in order to be a "monk." Indeed, this "separation" also goes hand in hand with the "harmonious union with all"! The following "beatitudes" teach us how Evagrius imagines this "harmonious union," which—as the biblical allusions make clear—hold true for all Christians who actually deserve this name.

> Blessed is the monk who regards all men as God after God. Blessed is the monk who willingly and with unmixed joy looks at everyone's salvation and progress as if they were his own. Blessed is the monk who sees himself as the offscouring of all things.[14]

*

[10]Eph 4:24; *In Ps.* 149:1 α.
[11]*Prologue to the Antirrhētikos* (*Ant. Prol.*) 7.
[12]*On Prayer* (*Or.*) 124.
[13]*Skemmata* (*Sk.*) 35.
[14]*Or.* 121–23.

For Evagrius, the historical man is a "spirit in a body" (νοῦς ἐνσώ-ματος)[15]: an immaterial, bodiless "spirit-soul" (νοῦς)[16] in a material, "practical" body[17] that serves as an "instrument" (ὄργανον) for the practice of the good—but also of evil.[18] With his spirit-soul "created in the image of God," man rises, so to speak, up into the divine world, while his material body links him with the sensory cosmos surrounding and "related" to him (and originating at the same time: συγγενής).[19]

While the body—like the entire material world—consists of four elements, the spirit-soul is composed of three "parts,"[20] and more precisely, since these actually constitute a unity, of three "powers" (δυνάμεις): the rational (λογιστικόν), the irascible (θυμικόν) and the concupiscible (ἐπιθυμητικόν).[21] The last two powers mentioned, which like the body we have in common with the animals,[22] are also summed up as the "irrational part" of the soul,[23] sometimes being called the "soul"[24] in general. The rational power, by contrast, is called the "intellect" (νοῦς). Each of these three powers has its own natural field of operation.

> The rational soul works according to nature when its concupiscible part desires virtue, the irascible does battle for it, and the rational devotes itself to a contemplation of the created.[25]

This harmony is possible only when all three powers work together not only "in accordance with nature"—i.e. according to the Creator's will—but also are in mutual agreement. When the irrational

---

[15] *Sk.* 14.
[16] *Gnostic Chapters (KG)* I.46.
[17] *Ibid.* IV.82.
[18] *Letters (Ep.)* 57.5
[19] *In Ps.* 43:20 ιβ.
[20] *KG* III.59.
[21] *Praktikos (Pr.)* 89.
[22] *KG* VI.85; *Sk.* 40; *On Various Evil Thoughts (M.c.)* 18.7 f.
[23] *Pr.* 84.
[24] *In Ps.* 107:3 β.
[25] *Pr.* 86.

part becomes independent, man loses his inner balance and falls victim to the passions.

> "Their anger is like that of the serpent": When the irascible power wins, the soul becomes "bestial"[26]; when desire wins, the soul becomes like a "horse" or a "mule."[27] If, on the contrary, the intellect is victorious, the soul becomes an angel,[28] or even God.[29]

In order to prevent the unnatural unrest of the intellect's "house companions"[30] and to unify the "inner triad through the bond of peace,"[31] order must rule among the three powers of the soul—that is, the intellect must take over the leadership belonging to it, for which reason it is also called the "governing" power (ἡγεμονικόν).[32] Then, as is already clear in the above-cited text, disorder always originates in the irrational part of the soul, called the "passionate part"[33] because it more than all others is prone to the passions, which Evagrius always understands as "diseases" (πάθη)[34] arising through the misuse of what is in itself good.[35] From this "passionate part" the disorder then spreads throughout the soul and "darkens the intellect."[36]

This proneness to the passions arises from the intimate connection between the two irrational powers and the body (and thereby material reality), which can trigger in us movements of desire and anger, but need not necessarily do so. In themselves, the material things of this world are good as creation and are in no way an obsta-

---

[26]Cf. Ps 48:13, 21.

[27]Ps 31:9. Cf. *In Ps.* 75:7 ζ. Horse and mule are biblical types of "passionate men who are irrationally driven to what is not seemly and neigh after the wives of their neighbors" (cf. Jer 5:8).

[28]Cf. *KG* I.68 (the intellect and fire prevail in an angel).

[29]*In Ps.* 57:5 β. On man as a "god," cf. *Ep. fid.* 3.8 ff. ("by grace"); *KG* IV.51, 81; *In Ps.* 5:7 γ (quotation 4, Ps 81:6).

[30]*Scholia on Proverbs* (*In Prov.*) 31:21 (G.377).

[31]Cf. *To Eulogius* (*Eul.*) 6.

[32]*In Ps.* 65:15 ζ.

[33]*In Ps.* 107:3 β.

[34]Cf. *KG* I.41.

[35]*Ibid.* III.59.

[36]*Pr.* 74.

cle on the way to salvation.[37] In general, therefore, the following is valid: "The passions are accustomed to be stirred up by the senses"[38]; "No impure thought arises in us without a sensory object."[39] However, the trigger of these impassioned movements lies within us[40] in our free "consent."[41]

> Those memories, colored by passion, that we find in ourselves come from former experiences we underwent while subject to some passion. Whatever experience we now undergo while under the influence of passion will in the future persist in us in the form of passionate memories.[42]

Additionally, one must note that in Evagrius' understanding, we are not dealing here with exclusively "psychological" processes within the soul, for the "passions of the soul also draw their momentum from people; those of the body, from the body"[43] and its natural needs. Yet standing invisibly[44] in the background are the demons, who through their temptations incite us to turn things that in themselves are natural into passions.[45] Only a truly unified and pacified soul is safe from these snares.

> The one whose intellect is always "with the Lord,"[46] whose irascible part is full of meekness owing to the remembrance of God, and whose desire completely inclines to the Lord, is entitled not to be afraid of our enemies who surround our body on all sides.[47]

*

---

[37] *In Ps.* 145:8 β.
[38] *Pr.* 38.
[39] *M.c.* 24.5.
[40] *Pr.* 6.
[41] *Ibid.* 75.
[42] *Ibid.* 34.
[43] *Ibid.* 35.
[44] *KG* I.22.
[45] *Pr.* 34.
[46] Ps 72:23.
[47] *KG* IV.73.

After these general statements, we must now determine more precisely the relationship between the two irrational powers as well as their respective relationship to the body and the intellect. Just as there are "psychic" and "physical" (literally: bodily) demons[48] who each attack the soul or the body, so too Evagrius distinguishes, as we have seen, between "passions of the soul" and "passions of the body" with a view to their respective causes. The driving force behind the latter is, as we have said, the "irrational part of the soul" which is closely connected with the body.

> "Prove me, O Lord, and try me; prove with fire my reins, and my heart": The "reins" are a symbol of the passionate part of the soul; that is, of the irascible and concupiscible; the "heart," on the contrary, is a symbol of the rational part.[49]

In another place, Evagrius distinguishes more precisely between irascibility and desire, and this differentiation allows us to understand better the key position which irascibility—as an irrational power and hence also the passions belonging to it—occupies in the totality of the human person.

> The irascible part of the soul is linked to the heart, where the rational [part] is also located; by contrast, its concupiscent part is bound up with "flesh and blood,"[50] inasmuch as we indeed[51] ought to "remove anger from the heart and malice from the flesh."[52]

The "passions of the body" arise from the body's natural needs,[53] such as nourishment, clothing, sexuality, and the like. These passions are, comparatively speaking, easily healed by the appropriate means[54]: above all, abstinence,[55] as the strict ascetic Evagrius confi-

---

[48] *Gn.* 31.
[49] *In Ps.* 25:2 α; cf. 72:21 ιδ; 107:3 β.
[50] I Cor 15:50.
[51] Cf. *Scholia on Ecclesiastes* (*In Eccl.*) 11:10 (G.72).
[52] *KG* IV.84.
[53] *Eul.* 23.
[54] *Pr.* 36.
[55] *Ibid.* 35.

dently declares. They are more "short-lived" than the passions of the soul.[56]

Passions of the soul are occasioned, of course, not only by our own person, but also by our relationship with our fellow human beings.[57] The passions arising from these interpersonal relationships—such as anger, rage, resentment, hatred, envy, jealousy, grudges, slander, but also vanity and pride—"last until old age."[58] Here, much stronger and costlier remedies are needed for the diseased "love of self" (φιλαυτία), this "one who hates all."[59] The chief of these remedies is "spiritual love"[60] in all its outward manifestations, such as meekness, forbearance, kindness, and others. Paul[61] rightly calls this love "great."[62]

It is easy to understand that the passions of the soul, though as such they are linked to the person of a fellow human being, can all too often be sparked by material objects these people possess or which are connected to them. They incite in some way our concupiscence, and this fuels anger.[63]

*

Within this framework, irascibility occupies a characteristic intermediate position. On the one hand, it belongs to "the passionate part of the soul," and on the other, it is also linked—just like the rational part—to the "heart," that is, to the intellect as the personal core of man. What happens, then, when irascibility, for whatever reason, is "inflamed?"

> Provoked irascibility blinds the beholder,[64]

that is, the intellect, the "intelligible eye" of the soul.[65] In particular, the passions of anger rob it of the divine "light"—that is, of percep-

---

[56]Cf. *Ep.* 25.3.
[57]*Pr.* 35.
[58]*Ep.* 25.3.
[59]*Maxims (Sent.)* 48.
[60]*Pr.* 35.
[61]1 Cor 13:13.
[62]*Pr.* 38.
[63]*Or.* 27.
[64]*KG* V.27.
[65]Cf. *Or.* 27.

tion[66]—and thus of its most inherent function.[67] Consequently the
converse is also true:

> Only when it is no longer determined[68] by thoughts of the passion-
> ate part of the soul does the intellect devote itself to intelligible
> realities.[69]

This is true above all for thoughts of the irascible part, which
occupies a key position between desire and the intellect. We will consider at length the sins of anger and their consequences, as well as the
appropriate means for healing them. Here, our concern has merely
been to get some idea of Evagrius' image of man in order to assess the
significance given to anger in that image.

☙   *

> When of all the powers of the soul, the rational part is the most pre-
> cious, and this part is only determined[70] by wisdom,[71] then wisdom
> is accordingly the first of all the virtues. Our wise teacher[72] in par-
> ticular also called wisdom "the spirit of sonship."[73]

Evagrius' image of man, like his spirituality, is clearly determined by
the primacy of the Spirit. At the center stands the "intellect" (νοῦς),
which is not to be equated with our *ratio* (reason) but—speaking bib-
lically—designates the "inner man"[74] created "in the image of God"[75]
and who also "in Christ"[76] through baptism has been "renewed

---

[66]*KG* VI.83.

[67]*In Ps.* 145:8 β.

[68]Ποιῶται = to receive a certain quality (ποιότης); used thus by Evagrius passim, cf. *Pr.* 30, 39, 42, 58; *Or.* 30.

[69]*KG* VI.55 (Greek text [Gr.]).

[70]See footnote 68 above.

[71]S1 reads "knowledge."

[72]Gregory Nazianzen, *Oration* 31.29; cf. *ibid.* 21.6.

[73]*KG* VI.51 Gr. Final quotation above: Rom 8:15.

[74]Cf. G. Bunge, "Nach dem Intellekt leben? Zum sogenannten 'Intellektualis-
mus' der evagrianischen Spiritualität," in *Simandron—Der Wachklopfer. Festschrift für
Klaus Gember*, ed. W. Nyssen (Cologne: 1989) 95–109.

[75]*In Ps.* 38:6 δ.

[76]*Ibid.* 44:4 γ.

according to the image of his Creator."[77] For only this "personal core"
of man is capable of having an "immediate"[78] relationship with God.
This primacy of the spiritual implies no depreciation of the body,
which Evagrius already forbade in his decisive position against the
Manichaean hostility towards the body.[79] As a result, he also does not
neglect the two "irrational powers" of the soul that are closely linked
to the body. Rather, the opposite is true, for Evagrius ascribes prominent meaning to the "health"[80] of this "passionate part" of the soul
precisely because his concern is the restoration of the rational part's
"natural operation." Since this "inner triad" forms a unity from which
no part can be removed—at least, not as long as we are in this body—
the "natural operation of the rational soul"[81] depends inescapably on
the ordered operation of precisely these two irrational powers.

> "Her husband is not concerned about the house companions when he
> is held up somewhere, for all who are with her are clothed": The intel-
> lect can neither forge ahead nor attain the contemplation of the incor-
> poreal if it has not put its inner business in order [beforehand]. For the
> disorder of the "house companions" [irascibility and desire] causes it
> to return to that place whence it had gone out. However, if it has
> achieved dispassion, it "lingers" in contemplation and "is not con-
> cerned about the house companions." For irascibility is "attired" with
> meekness and humility, and desire with prudence and abstinence.[82]

The goal of impassibility is nothing less than a restoration of the
natural operation *of all three powers of the soul* in accordance with their
creation. Consequently, it is no wonder that the demons do everything in their power to prevent precisely this.

> When our irascibility is aroused in a way contrary to nature, it greatly
> helps the aim of the demons and their evil intrigues. Therefore, none

---

[77]*M.c.* 3.35; *Ep. Mel.* 16.
[78]*Or.* 3
[79]Cf. *KG* IV.60; *In Prov.* 20:12 (G.215).
[80]Cf. *Pr.* 56.
[81]*Ibid.* 86.
[82]*In Prov.* 31:21 (G.377).

of them refuses a chance to provoke it day and night. But when they see it tethered by meekness, they set it free at once on some [seem-ingly] proper pretext, so that having excited [this irascibility] most violently, they can use it for their bestial thoughts.[83] For this reason it is necessary not to let it get excited whether for right or wrong rea-sons, lest we furnish the [demons] who awe [us thereby] with an evil broadsword. Many do this, I know, and people become worked up more than is seemly for the most insignificant of reasons.[84]

Certainly the demons attempt to lead us astray into all passions, but they seem to have a special relationship to that of anger. Why is this so? We must now investigate this question.

---

[83]Anger is the "watchdog" of the soul (cf. *M.c.* 5.14, 25 ff.; *Sk.* 9, 10), which one must keep tied to a leash.

[84]*M.c.* 5.1–12.

CHAPTER 2

The Vice of Demons

H ad one asked Evagrius which vice, in his opinion, would unquestionably be the worst of all and have the most far-reaching effects on the spiritual life, he would have answered without hesitation: anger, and for this simple reason: "No other evil makes man in particular as much like a demon as anger."[1]

Certainly, all vices are ultimately of demonic origin. Yet the last two on the list of the eight "generic thoughts"[2]—vainglory and arrogance—are not only the passions we feel to be most odious; they also possess a distinctly "demonic" character. Vainglory is, of course, intimately linked to pride, "the devil's first offspring."[3] What is more, "pride is that arch-evil that flung to earth[4] 'Lucifer [himself] who rises early in the morning.'"[5] Accordingly, human pride along with its companion, vainglory, is primarily a vice of the perfect, who imagine that they have been able to scale the heights of the spiritual life by their own might. It thus appears for the most part only at the end in order to cause then the greatest fall, including hallucinations. Interestingly, such a fall is often followed by anger,[6] a fact that also manifests the common "demonic" character of the two vices. But anger itself, while being a perversion of one of our natural powers,[7] lies in wait for man at all levels of the spiritual life. What makes it so unmistakably "demonic"?

---

[1] *Ep.* 56.4 Gr.
[2] *Pr.* 6. See under Chapter 3.
[3] *M.c.* 1.12.
[4] Is 14:12.
[5] *Pr.* Prologue (21).
[6] *Ibid.* 14.
[7] *KG* III.59.

A demon is a rational nature, which, because of an abundance of anger, has fallen away from the ascetic life (πρακτική).[8]

It only follows that Evagrius should laconically declare: "The one who masters anger has mastery over the demons."[9] The abovementioned definition may be explained as follows: in every being endowed with reason—angel, man, or demon—there is a "predominant" quality determining all its behavior. In a demon, this quality is precisely "irascibility" (θυμός), as Evagrius garners from Holy Scripture— always understood in "an intelligible and spiritual sense"[10]:

> "God . . . my deliverer from my raging enemies": Those in whom anger predominates also have rage predominating in them. But when our "enemies are raging," our enemies are also angry. It is said[11]: "Their anger resembles that of the serpent,"[12] and "when their anger raged against us."[13]

The "enemies" are of course the demons "in whom the irascible part predominates."[14] This wickedness is by no means theirs by nature[15]; otherwise, God himself would be the author of evil. On the contrary, it is the result of an "evil decision of the will" that wrought this "change" in their existence. Consequently, they became the "adverse powers."[16] In Evagrius' understanding, anger—like any vice—is not at all "natural," but "contranatural," opposed to its own created nature!

Accordingly, the wickedness of a "reason-endowed being," and therefore of man, is not found in his "being" (οὐσία) but always in his "behavior" (ἕξις), which is a quality[17] (ποιότης) one can acquire (or also lose). Since by "contranatural anger"[18] we mean, as was said, a

---

[8]*Ibid.* 34.
[9]*M.c.* 13.1.
[10]*In Prov.* 23:1, 3 (G.251).
[11]Ps 57:5.
[12]Ps 123:3.
[13]*In Ps.* 17:49 κε.
[14]*In Prov.* 5:9 (G.60); cf. *KG* I.68 et passim.
[15]*KG* V.47.
[16]*Ep. fid.* 10.15 ff.; cf. *In Prov.* 2:17 (G.23).
[17]*In Ps.* 70:4 β.
[18]*Pr.* 24.

misuse of a power good in itself,[19] a man can consequently become a demon through his evil way of life, be it after death[20] or already in his lifetime.

> When we are formed in the womb, we live the life of plants; when born, that of animals; and when grown up, that of angels or demons. The foundation of the first life is the animated substance; that of the second, the senses; that of the third, the fact that we are prone not only to virtue but also to vice.[21]

With this statement, Evagrius emphatically declares—again apologetically against dualism—that we carry in us since our creation the "seeds of virtue," but not those of vice.[22] As said above, the latter arise from an "evil decision of the will." God alone is essentially good and incapable of anything opposite[23]; by contrast, each rational nature is "susceptible to opposition,"[24] since it has received not only its being but also its condition of being good. But being susceptible entails changeability,[25] the ability to improve one's own "condition" but also to worsen it, in that on the basis of his conduct—of his life— man becomes an "angel" or a "demon." "Think not that a demon is anything else but a man filled with anger who eludes our sense perception!"[26]

For the demons also have a body, as it were, even if its composition is of a different type than that of ours (thus escaping our sense perception). What appears as a demon to many people is nothing more than an illusion, an alien body adopted for deception.[27]

*

---

[19] Cf. *KG* III.59.
[20] Cf. *ibid.* V.11; *In Ps.* 1:5 et passim.
[21] *KG* III.76 Gr. and Syr.
[22] *Ibid.* I.39.
[23] *Ibid.* 1.
[24] *Ibid.* 64.
[25] *Ep. fid.* 10.15.
[26] *Ep.* 56.4.
[27] *KG* I.22; V.18.

The one who abstains from food and drink, but provokes anger because of evil thoughts, is like a ship on the high seas with a demon for a pilot.[28]

This insight is easily understood. After what has been said, however, it has become clear that a man who allows himself to be ruled by the demonic vice of anger becomes a "demon" through this behavior of his. Here too as always, Evagrius refers to Holy Scripture. "'The wine drinkers sang about me to the music of strings': This 'wine' means[29] the 'anger of dragons.'"[30]

Hence anger is that "dragon's wine"[31] from which the true "Nazirite," the monk, must altogether abstain,[32] as Evagrius evinces from Numbers 6:3.

"Wine is an unruly thing and inebriation is brazen": If the "anger of dragons is their wine,"[33] but "wine is an unruly thing," then anger is an unruly thing that makes people unruly, and rage is "brazen." This inebriation is wont to come about through the boiling of the irascible power. Yet if the Nazirites refrain from wine according to the Law, then the Nazirites are also required to be free of anger.[34]

Certainly, it is general knowledge that one can "boil with rage." But very few consider that one can become not only drunk from this high-percentage "dragon's wine," but can also become a "serpent"[35] or demon. In this context, the utterance about "animal rage" comes unconsciously quite close to reality.

" 'Their anger is like that of the serpent': If anger triumphs, then the soul becomes brutish,"[36] that is, it becomes a demon.[37] Indeed,

---

[28]*M.c.* 13.15–18.
[29]Cf. Job 20:16.
[30]*In Ps.* 68:13 η.
[31]Cf. Deut 32:33.
[32]*KG* V.44.
[33]Deut 32:33.
[34]*In Prov.* 20:1 (G.206).
[35]*Ep.* 56.5.
[36]*In Ps.* 57:5 β.
[37]*KG* I.53.

the "wild animal" (θηρίον) is the biblical symbol for a demon, whose "predominant" characteristic is precisely the wild, bestial and thus irrational anger.

> "Do not deliver the soul that acknowledges you to the wild animals": If the demons are called "wild animals," and anger prevails in wild animals, then anger also prevails in demons. In Job it also says[38]: "The wild animals of the field will be at peace with you."[39]

While the goal of the spiritual life is to elevate man to "an almost angelic condition,"[40] even to make him "angel-like,"[41] anger lowers him below his natural state, "renders him bestial" (ἀποθηριοῖ) and turns him into a "demon."

* * *

The allegorical interpretation of Scripture, to which Evagrius owes his insights on the essence of demons and the metamorphosis of man into a demon, is for many modern readers perhaps no longer readily accessible. Nevertheless, in a letter Evagrius points to a context that even today commands our attention. He admonishes a certain Aedesius to "subdue his anger, which is a 'Judas' who delivers the intellect to the demons."[42] Meant here is Judas Iscariot, one of the twelve apostles[43] chosen by Christ himself,[44] the one whom the Lord, in a dramatic moment and with an eye to his later betrayal, called a "demon"![45]

This betrayal of Judas is a mysterious event that already moved the first Christians very deeply, and is disturbing even today. Evagrius now implies that Judas delivered the Lord to his deadly enemies out of anger. How can he arrive at this? Let us inquire what the Gospels themselves say about Judas.

---

[38]Job 5:23.
[39]*In Ps.* 73:19 θ.
[40]*Ibid.* 118:171 οθ.
[41]*Or.* 113; see under Chapter 9.
[42]*Ep.* 6.4.
[43]Matt 26:14 et passim.
[44]John 6:70.
[45]*Ibid.* ff.

*

As "one of the Twelve," Judas Iscariot belonged to that small group of followers who were especially close to Jesus. The Lord entrusted to these Twelve much that he explained to "the others"—the "outsiders"—only in parables.[46] They accompanied him throughout the entire period of his public activity, thereby becoming his privileged witnesses. Judas left this group on his own impulse shortly before Jesus' death, for which he himself was to blame in that he betrayed and sold the Master to the high priests.[47]

In this context, a word found in the Gospel of Luke suddenly throws a glaring light upon the dark background of this betrayal. "Then Satan entered into Judas . . . "[48] In the Gospel of John also the text reads, "The devil had put it into Judas' heart to betray [the Lord]."[49] A little later, during the Last Supper, it is stated again that Satan had "entered" Judas when he accepted the morsel from the Lord's hand.[50]

Thus, the evangelists Luke and John are of the opinion that the one who actually manipulated the betrayal was "Satan," "the devil," that "murderer from the beginning" whom Christ accordingly designates as the actual "father" of those Jews wishing to murder him.[51] Yet how has it come about that Satan found precisely in Judas the tool required for his murder of the "second Adam"? In general, what happens when a man becomes a demon? The question must be asked, for Judas is not the only one whom Christ designates as a devil. In a no less dramatic moment, he also called Peter "Satan"—one of the three apostles who stood closest to him![52]

The case of Peter gives us an important clue to understanding this frightening event. When Jesus speaks for the first time openly about his impending Passion, Peter tries—with the best intentions, it

---

[46]Mark 4:11.
[47]Matt 26:14 ff. par.
[48]Luke 22:3.
[49]John 13:2.
[50]*Ibid.* 13:27.
[51]*Ibid.* 8:44.
[52]Matt 16:23 par.

seems—to hold him back from this. Consequently, Christ rebukes him and calls him Satan because he is "thinking not as God thinks but as men do!"[53] This same context is also assumed in John. When Jesus, in his famous "hard word," alludes in a hardly veiled manner to his approaching violent death, many disciples are shocked and leave him. Peter then commits himself to him in the name of the Twelve as "the Holy One of God." Christ indicates, however, that Judas—who had not left him—has already lost his faith and has become "a devil."[54]

Accordingly, the stumbling block for all the disciples[55]—and not merely for Peter and Judas—is the *passio Christi*: the Cross. They saw in Christ above all a purely "human," intramundane Messiah, a political liberator of Israel, linking to this "faith" very selfish expectations: not only Judas, about whose greed we hear,[56] and Peter; but also, for example, the two sons of Zebedee.[57] Such political expectations appear as "human" to us and therefore pardonable. Christ, on the other hand, calls them "satanic" and "demonic" since they are contrary to God. In like manner, the apostle speaks of a "wisdom" that is "earthly, sensuous, and demonic"[58]—everything on one and the same level.

* * *

Let us return again to Evagrius. The fact that Christ himself, in a decisive moment in which the essence of his own mission was at stake, respectively calls Peter and Judas Iscariot "Satan" and a "devil"—since they entirely misunderstood this mission, going so far as to try to lead him away from his path—brings us to the secret motive of Judas' betrayal. That high angelic being that once occupied an enviable place under "the trees of Paradise"[59] fell, "forfeit[ing] his

---

[53]*Ibid.*
[54]John 6:70 f.
[55]Luke 8:23; 24:21.
[56]Matt 26:15 par.; John 12:6.
[57]Matt 20:20 ff.
[58]Jas 3:15.
[59]Ezek 31:9.

angelic dignity and becom[ing] a devil"[60] because he gave himself over to the vice of pride (ὑπερηφανία) and said: "I shall set my throne above the stars. I shall be like the Most High!"[61] Instead of recognizing his own creatureliness in "thankful confession of God" and a "true recognition of nature," and instead of recognizing "humbly [in] a stark admission [his] weakness"[62]—that one's own holiness is an "obtained" good,[63] and not one's own property—this leader of the angels exalted himself not only above the "stars," but in a grotesque manner even above his Creator. And he who wanted "to be like the Most High" also seduced man, destined to be "like God,"[64] into desiring to be "like God" by his own might![65]

That being, then, who made "the beginning" of that "movement"[66] and who hurled "the seal of likeness and the crown of beauty"[67] from heaven to earth,[68] now reveals the secret driving force behind his "evil decision of the will." He is "enflamed with great anger"[69] and his symbol is the "serpent," the "dragon." His hatred is directed first at the "second Adam"[70] who came to raise up the "fallen image"[71] and to lead it to its original destiny, the "likeness to God."[72] As soon as the devil catches sight of him, he pressures him who said of himself, "I am gentle and humble in heart,"[73] to betray his true mission and establish his kingdom by his own authority in this world: first in person[74] and then through his most trusted disciples. The anger and "envy"[75] of the fallen

---

[60]*Ep. fid.* 10:15 ff.
[61]Is 14:12 f.; cf. *In Prov.* 2:17 (G.23).
[62]*Vita Supplementa*, ed. J. Muyldermans. *Le Muséon* 54 (1941): 5.
[63]*Ep. fid.* 10:17 f.
[64]Gen 1:26; 1 John 3:2.
[65]Gen 3:5.
[66]*KG* VI.36.
[67]Ezek 28:12.
[68]*M.c.* 14:11 ff.
[69]Rev 12:12.
[70]Cf. 1 Cor 15:45.
[71]*Gn* 50.
[72]*Ep. Mel.* 62.
[73]Matt 11:29.
[74]Matt 4:1 ff.; cf. *M.c.* 1.17 ff.
[75]Wis 2:24.

prince of the angels are then directed against all those whom the Messiah, who is "gentle and humble in heart," will redeem through his perfect self-emptying even to the cross.[76] The devil found his first victim in Judas. How so?

*

We have seen already that there exists a secret connection between pride and anger. Such a link also exists, however, between pride and avarice, that vice to which Judas had yielded, according to the testimony of the Evangelists. Evagrius finds a hint of this connection in the temptation story of Jesus himself.

> No one escapes pride, the first offspring of the devil, unless one has banished "avarice, the root of all evil,"[77] since, according to Solomon the wise,[78] "poverty makes a man humble."[79]

Avarice belongs to the three temptations by which the devil sought to make Christ fall in the desert. The one who yields to them—or to one of them—becomes prone to the others![80] This now also clarifies Judas Iscariot's fall.

> "Let the devil now stand to his right": Satan stood at the right of those whose "right" works he cuts off. In Zechariah it reads: "And the Lord showed me Joshua, the high priest, standing before the presence of the Angel of the Lord, and the devil stood at his right hand"—not in general, but "to resist him."[81] But he does not "resist" Judas,[82]

for Judas "had no clean hands, nor was his heart pure. He was namely a thief and took away what was laid aside."[83] The life—Christ[84]—that he too carried in himself, "and the intelligible riches and the spiritual

---

[76]Phil 2:6 ff.
[77]1 Tim 6:10.
[78]Prov 10:4.
[79]*M.c.* 1.11–14.
[80]*Ibid.* 15 ff.
[81]Zech 3:1.
[82]*In Ps.* 108:6 γ.
[83]John 12:6; cf. *In Ps.* 23:3–4 β.
[84]John 14:6.

goods" which had been bestowed on him as well, were of no use to him, "since he had betrayed the wisdom and the truth of God for the sake of gain."[85] However, he did this not only on account of the thirty pieces of silver, but because he was driven by the devil's anger and pride, to whom greed, this "mother of idolatry,"[86] had delivered him.

*

Peter and Judas Iscariot were both indignant—though for different reasons—at the thought of a suffering Messiah. The idea that Jesus would not be the hoped-for political "King of Israel," but would end up on the cross, deeply wounded their "self-love" (φιλαυτία), in which Evagrius sees the hidden root of all the passions[87]—even that of anger and pride, which he draws closely together.[88] Since this self-love is only "a friend to itself," Evagrius fittingly calls it the "hater of all."[89]

At this point, however, the two apostles part ways. Despite dangerous oscillations, Peter remains faithful to his Lord, while Judas delivers him to his deadly enemies. Two things are characteristic of the proud man. He is marked by a self-overestimation allowing him to deny God's help and ascribe to himself what has been accomplished, and a disdain for others who are unable to appreciate his own greatness.[90] Once again, anger is the hidden motive of his contempt.

It is easy to see how the proud man can transfer his dreams of omnipotence to others, whose "prophet" he then becomes and in whose retinue he himself hopes to become great. One only has to think of "the places on the right and the left." If these vain expectations are disappointed—and this disappointment was prepared for the disciples by their suffering Messiah Jesus—then anger appears[91] and the wounded love of self suddenly turns into hatred for the "one who failed" and who must now be destroyed. That Judas then literally sells

---

[85]*In Eccl.* 5:17–19 (G.43).
[86]Col 3:5; cf. *Ep.* 27.5; *Pr.* Prologue (41).
[87]*Sk.* 53.
[88]*Pr.* 14.
[89]*Sk.* 48.
[90]*Pr.* 14.
[91]*Ibid.*

the Lord proves that he was already enslaved to one of the basest but most serious vices: greed. *Philargyria* is not simply mere stinginess, but (literally) "love of silver," of money. Why does the miser love money? Ultimately it serves him only as a means to an end, namely, as the means to achieving his own ambitious and proud desires. Power needs money, and money strives for power—the power that enslaves the other and which Christ, who of his own will became poor,[92] consciously refused when the devil offered it to him in the desert.

With the destruction of Christ, "the one who was a murderer from the beginning"[93] has not yet completed his work. When Judas sees how the matter will come to an end, he does not, for instance, shed bitter tears of repentance like Peter (as when the latter shamefully denied his Lord and became aware of his deed[94]). Rather, true to his own self-overestimation, he attempts by his own might to undo what had been done.[95] When this proves to be impossible, he takes his own life,[96] since sadness and despair arise as a result of disappointed pride after anger. Then the final evil comes: mental disturbance and demonic visions.[97] After Satan has ended his work, he can discard his disguise.

In this uncanny manner, the parallel between the tempter and the tempted is fulfilled. Just as the lofty prince of the angels lost his preeminent place under the "trees of Paradise" on account of pride, so too does Judas on account of pride lose his chosen place among the twelve Apostles.[98]

Consequently, the sins of a misguided irascibility are something truly frightening. "The one who has become a slave of this passion is absolutely alien to the monastic life" and has nothing in common with the "ways of our Redeemer."[99] His supposed "spiritual life," espe-

---

[92] 2 Cor 8:9.
[93] John 8:44.
[94] Matt 26:75.
[95] *Ibid.* 27:3 ff.
[96] *Ibid.* 27:5.
[97] *Pr.* 14.
[98] Acts 1:16 ff.
[99] *M.c.* 13.2 ff.

cially his prayer, is nothing but a mimicry of reality, provoking God's anger against the insolent man.[100] Whoever wants to pray in this frame of mind resembles a man who would like to see clearly and puts out his own eyes.[101] Indeed, how could such a "demon" even pray? It is profitable to investigate in greater detail this vice, all too frequently misunderstood since it is easily underestimated.

---

[100] *Or.* 145, 146.
[101] *Ibid.* 64.

CHAPTER 3

Anger in the List of the Eight Evil Thoughts

L ike other Fathers of his time, Evagrius also professes the absolute ontological priority of good—in conscious opposition to the Manichaean dualism that was apparently quite widespread in his surroundings.

> There was a time when evil did not exist, and the time will come when it will exist no more. However, there was never a time when virtue did not exist and there will be no time when it will no longer be . . .[1]

For evil (κακία) is ontologically of a secondary nature.[2] It arises through the perversion of a being that is a good in itself, and it subsists only as long as this perversion continues. Even if the two irrational powers, irascibility and desire, being tied to "flesh and blood"—the ephemeral material body—in relation to man's spiritual being (the intellect), are likewise for Evagrius of an ontologically secondary nature,[3] nonetheless the fact remains that they are willed by the Creator and are therefore good. Their misuse alone is evil, and from this ensues what we call "vice": πάθος—suffering/passion.

> If every evil is wont to arise out of the rational, concupiscent, and irascible part, and one can use this power for good as well as for evil, then the vices apparently befall us through the contranatural use of

---

[1] *KG* I.40 Gr.
[2] *Ibid.* I.39.
[3] *Ibid.* VI.85.

these parts [of the soul]. But if this is the case, then nothing that comes from God is evil [in itself].[4]

The same also applies to the things of this creation and their images (ὁμοιώματα) in our mind, the "mental representations" (νοήματα) they leave behind like "imprints" in our intellect.[5]

"The Lord sets the chained ones free": Neither things nor their mental conceptions [as such] chain the intellect, but, on the contrary, the passionate conceptions of things. For the Lord has also made gold, and he himself created woman, and nothing of what has come into existence through God is opposed to the salvation of man. On the contrary, it is lust and greed that chain the intellect, in that they force the mental conceptions to remain in the heart. Things hamper the intellect through passionate mental conceptions, just as [the thought of] water [hampers] the thirsty man through thirst and [the thought of] bread the hungry man through hunger. For this reason, the physician of souls neither destroys things (for he is their Creator) nor does he compel the intellect not to recognize them (for it was created by him for this reason, to recognize them). Rather, by destroying by means of spiritual teaching and the commandments the passions—which are something other than the mental representations and the things from which they have their origin—he frees the intellect from the chains. This is indeed what the words of the Psalm mean: "The Lord sets the chained ones free."[6]

*

Throughout his life, Evagrius studied these impassioned "thoughts"; he analyzed them and sought to arrange them in order so as to facilitate for himself and his readers the very important "discernment of spirits."[7] At the end is found a list of eight so-called "generic thoughts," whose ultimate root is *philautia*,[8] or "love of self."

---

[4]*Ibid.* III.59.
[5]*M.c.* 25.
[6]*In Ps.* 145:8 β.
[7]*Ep.* 4.4, 5.
[8]*Sk.* 53.

There are eight classes of thoughts in which every thought is contained. The first is gluttony, followed by lust. The third is greed, the fourth sadness. The fifth is anger, the sixth acedia; the seventh is vainglory and the eighth is pride. Whether all of these disturb the soul or not, does not depend upon us; but whether they linger or do not linger, arouse the passions or not—this depends on us.[9]

All remaining thoughts—being various manifestations of one of these basic types—can be traced back to these eight generic thoughts. In the case of irascibility, these are envy and censoriousness,[10] mistrust,[11] hatred, rancor, evil slander[12] and more of the same. Although Evagrius himself does not seem to have worked out a systematic assignation of these eight thoughts to one of the soul's three powers, one can easily imagine how such thoughts might be assigned. Gluttony, lust, and greed are clearly "vices of the body,"[13] arising from its misguided needs, and can be assigned pre-eminently to desire. Sorrow, anger, and acedia are "vices of the soul,"[14] often having their cause in the domain of interpersonal relationships—but certainly this is not always or exclusively the case. We shall see, of course, that these eight thoughts also merge with one another and/or grow out of each other. The three named vices can be classified as the inappropriate behavior of the irascible power, but from the example of acedia, it becomes clear why Evagrius himself did not carry through such a systematic assignation that would lead thus to simplification. Acedia arises out of a simultaneous movement of desire and irascibility.[15] The last two vices, vainglory and pride, may be assigned to the soul's rational part. Additionally, according to Evagrius we hold the first six thoughts in common with the animals, because they assail the soul's irrational part, while the last two are typically human passions and

---

[9]Cf. *Pr.* 6.
[10]*M.c.* 18.4.
[11]*Ibid.* 32.4.
[12]*Gn.* 32.
[13]Cf. *Pr.* 35.
[14]*Ibid.*
[15]*In Ps.* 118:28 ιγ, 139:3 α.

tend to strike only "rational natures."[16] Accordingly, they are also the
typical vices of the perfect.[17]

*

The correlations between these eight generic thoughts are extremely
varied; indeed, it is very difficult to present them exhaustively. Moreover, nowhere does Evagrius attempt this. Rather, he establishes certain principles by which one can find one's bearings. This is written
programmatically right in the first chapter of the treatise *On Thoughts*:

> Among the demons opposing us in the ascetic life (πρακτική), the
> first to begin combat in battle are those who are entrusted with the
> cravings of gluttony, those who instill greed within us, and those
> who entice us to seek human glory. All the others march behind
> them and gather those who have been wounded by them.
>
> For it is not possible to fall into the hands of the demon of lust,
> unless one has first fallen to the demon of gluttony. And it is not pos-
> sible to arouse anger unless one is fighting for food, possessions, or
> honor. And it is not possible to escape the demon of sadness, unless
> [one remains unmoved] on being deprived of all these things or on
> being unable to acquire them. Nor is man able to escape pride, the
> devil's first offspring, unless he has banished "avarice, the root of all
> evil"[18] since, according to Solomon the wise, "poverty makes a man
> humble."[19]
>
> In short, it is not possible for man to fall into the power of a
> demon, unless he has first been wounded by those first troops [i.e. the
> vices]. This is why the devil, at one time, suggested these three
> thoughts to the Savior: first, he asked him to turn stones into bread;
> then he promised him the entire world, if he would fall down and wor-
> ship him; and thirdly, he said that if he would listen to him, he would
> be glorified, because he would not suffer any injury from such a fall.[20]

---

[16]*M.c.* 18:1 ff.
[17]Cf. *Pr.* 13.
[18]1 Tim 6:10.
[19]Prov 10:4.
[20]Matt 4:1–10.

But our Lord, showing himself superior to these temptations, ordered the devil to withdraw. In this way he taught us that it is not possible to drive away the devil, unless we scorn these three thoughts.[21]

From the style and manner in which Christ stopped the mouth of the tempter—that is, by hurling back at him each time a word from Holy Scripture—Evagrius derives his own method of *antirrhēsis* or "counter-statement" for the battle against tempting thoughts.[22]

From what has been said, an interesting observation arises: "The demons do not tempt us all simultaneously," since our intellect, despite its own swiftness, cannot "grasp at one and the same time the thoughts of two things." It fixes its attention in each instance on one object only, which moreover is always of a sensory nature. Consequently, unclean thoughts of greed and rancor do not assail us simultaneously, because the intellect is unable to grasp at the same time the mental image (νόημα) of gold and that of the person who has chagrined us.[23]

Thus, as a general rule it holds true that the "thoughts" and the demons making use of them[24] follow one another. The knowledge of this sequence is a science, the foundations of which (aside from our own observation[25]) only Christ can lay.[26] Let us take a closer look at these "foundations" or "reasons" (λόγοι) in so far as Evagrius has disclosed them. "Wrath" (ὀργή) is a misdirected, perverted working of the irrational "irascible" (θυμικόν) power of the soul, which itself is simply called "anger" (θυμός). Anger and wrath have, as it were, both primary and secondary causes and results. A primary cause can be, for example, an injustice one has suffered, an insult (true or imagined),[27] unjust slander,[28] a groundless reprimand,[29] or even persecutions[30] and

---

[21]*M.c.* 1.
[22]*Ant. Prol.* Cf. our translation and commentary.
[23]*M.c.* 24.
[24]*Eul.* 15.
[25]Cf. *M.c.* 8; *Pr.* 51.
[26]*Pr.* 50.
[27]*Ibid.* 11.
[28]*Antirrhētikos (Ant.)* V.4, 11.
[29]*Ibid.* 23.
[30]*Ibid.* 34.

blows.[31] Whatever one has suffered generates anger and wrath, both of which yearn for vengeance. If this vengefulness is not satisfied, sadness—a feeling of frustration—manifests itself.[32]

A provoked anger, however, also spurs its victim on to deeds triggering the same stirrings in others. These include: lying and false witness,[33] calumny[34] or simply indignant murmuring,[35] suspicions,[36] the desire to write something insulting to the other,[37] the refusal to be reconciled,[38] and more of the sort. In short, anger urges one to "repay evil with evil."[39] In all this, the demon is not disconcerted at subtle arguments as the following text teaches, which many a person will have already experienced as an inner monologue. At the same time, this citation offers an example of the manner in which the abovementioned "antirrhetical method" is put to practical use.

> [Speak] to the thoughts of anger, which do not permit us to be reconciled to our brothers by putting before our eyes appropriate reasons, which are: shame, fear, and pride—ostensibly "lest he who erred in these previous transgressions fall into the same again." But this is a sign of the perfidy of the demon who will not permit the intellect to be free of resentment: "Do not let the sun go down on your anger, and give no opportunity to the devil."[40]

A secondary cause of anger, appearing in this case as the result of another passion, is pride, as we saw in the preceding chapter. For the overbearing man's imaginings of omnipotence do not shatter at the refusal of others to follow him. Frustration then generates rage and resentment, from which (for the abovementioned reasons) follows grief, and sometimes even worse things: insanity and hallucina-

---

[31]*Ibid.* 36.
[32]*Pr.* 10; *On the Eight Evil Spirits (O.Sp.)* 5.1.
[33]*Ant.* V.3.
[34]*Ibid.* 5.
[35]*Or.* 12.
[36]*Ant.* V.10.
[37]*Ibid.* 32.
[38]*Ibid.* 28.
[39]*Ibid.* 42, 53, 61.
[40]*Ibid.* 49. Quotation: Eph 4:26.

tions.[41] A widespread secondary cause of anger is formed by the cravings "which supply anger its material."[42]

An example of this is the desire for possessions and wealth,[43] which can produce hatred for others who stand in one's way. Since monks lived in voluntary poverty, albeit a poverty not always willingly endured, Evagrius mentions this cause repeatedly.[44]

*

Meanwhile, it is not even necessary that we ourselves be directly concerned. Stirrings of anger can also arise from so-called "natural" thoughts found in our created nature and hence also good, such as concern for our relatives.[45] It is not even necessary that these concerns be at all substantiated; it is easy for the demons to lead us to believe that those who are close to us are in danger.

> The demon of anger also mimics this demon [of lust] and forms [in our mind the image] of our parents, friends, and relatives, who are being insulted by contemptible people and are being beaten, thus provoking the anger of the anchorites in order that they might say or do something vicious to the [figures] that appear in their mind. We must be on our guard against this and snatch our mind away from such images as quickly as possible, lest it become a "smoldering stump"[46] at the time of prayer on account of dallying with them. People prone to anger are liable to fall into these temptations, and especially those who are easily inflamed into outbursts of anger. They are far from pure prayer and from the knowledge of Christ our Redeemer![47]

A most peculiar relationship exists between irascibility, which in this case is always active in conjunction with desire, and the vice of

---

[41] *Pr.* 14.
[42] *Or.* 27.
[43] *M.c.* 1.
[44] *Ant.* V.15, 30; *Ep.* 39:4; *To the Monks* (*Mn.*) 16 et passim.
[45] *Sk.* 56; *Ep.* 55.3 f.
[46] Is 7:4.
[47] *M.c.* 16.22 ff.

weariness of soul, or acedia. "Acedia is a simultaneous and perduring stirring of irascibility and desire, whereby the former is angry about what is at hand, while the latter yearns for what is not present . . ."[48]

In the case of acedia, thoughts of anger and desire combine (literally "interweave") to form a peculiar phenomenon that turns its victim into an "irrational animal . . . reared by desire and beaten by hatred."[49] The thought of acedia is so extensive that "on this day no other thought comes after it; first, because it persists, and then also since it contains nearly all thoughts in itself."[50]

The above explains why thoughts of acedia can appear in apparently such contradictory ways: in the lukewarm, as sluggishness, indifference, and even depression, and in the conscientious and eager, as unrestrained activism and ascetical maximalism. If this vice is not healed by steadfast endurance and a life of discipline, combined with "tears before God" and constant short prayers, it leads to a complete standstill of the spiritual life and sometimes even suicide. Yet he who bravely and steadfastly passes the trials of this "noonday demon," who "encompasses the entire soul and [threatens] to oppress the spirit,"[51] emerges from these tests inwardly strengthened. Unexpectedly, those spiritual experiences from which he thought himself forever to be excluded are now revealed to him.[52]

---

[48] *In Ps.* 118:28 ιγ.
[49] *Ep.* 27.6 Gr.
[50] *In Ps.* 139:3 α.
[51] *Pr.* 36.
[52] On this topic, cf. G. Bunge, *Akedia. Die geistliche Lehre des Evagrios Pontikos vom Überdruß* (Würzburg: Der christliche Osten, 1995⁴).

CHAPTER 4

The Essential Definition of Vice

According to Evagrius' understanding, all vices arise from a per-version of the activities—good in themselves—of the soul's three powers. Thus, in opposition to a working "according to nature" (that is, a functioning that is in agreement with God's original cre-ative will and thus of primary order), there arises an "unnatural" and secondary working. "The rational soul operates according to nature when the following conditions are realized: the concupiscible part desires virtue; the irascible part fights to obtain it; the rational part, finally, applies itself to the contemplation of created things."[1]

Consequently, irascibility naturally has a combative essence. The virtues proper to it, then, are courage (or manliness, ἀνδρεία), perse-verance,[2] and that specifically Christian love[3]—that virtue of the mighty that manifests itself as meekness, as the examples of Moses,[4] David,[5] and Christ[6] teach us, whom Scripture describes to us as "meek."

The object of this love that places the self in the background is the neighbor. He is still the neighbor even if the demons should have defiled this "likeness of God,"[7] since man always remains lovable, even as a sinner, precisely on account of being in the "image and like-ness of God."[8]

---

[1]*Pr.* 86.
[2]*Ibid.* 89.
[3]*Gn.* 47.
[4]Num 12:3.
[5]Ps 131:1.
[6]Matt 11:29.
[7]*Pr.* 89.
[8]*In Ps.* 118:113 v.

The demons attack this image by turning our legitimate anger against sin into anger against the sinner—against whom no anger can be justified.[9] Any apparently justifiable grounds for such anger are always merely "pretexts."[10] The entire unnaturalness of this anger against our neighbor becomes clear upon reflecting that "it is the nature of anger to fight the demons,"[11] and, as the case may be, their "thoughts."[12] Such anger does not harm the soul in the least[13]—quite the opposite. On the contrary, this is that "perfect hatred"[14] which Evagrius viewed as a "sign of the first and greatest dispassion"![15]

Metaphorically speaking, irascibility is, as it were, the soul's "hound." His task is "to kill only the wolves [that is, the demons], and not to devour the sheep; but rather 'to show the greatest gentleness to all men.'"[16] For "irascibility is a power of the soul that destroys thought [in a pejorative sense],"[17] in that it—like a faithful watchdog—"chases away all passions"[18] and "pursues the unjust."[19] When man wields all his aggressiveness against the demons, he acts entirely "according to nature" (κατὰ φύσιν).[20] However, Evagrius is careful to point out that "we revile the demons on account of the evil within them," but not insofar as they are God's creatures,[21] for they are "not evil in essence"[22] and were not created as such by God.

*

---

[9] *Or.* 24.
[10] Cf. *Pr.* 22.
[11] *Ibid.* 24.
[12] *M.c.* 16.16 ff.
[13] *Pr.* 93.
[14] Ps 138:22.
[15] *M.c.* 10.14 f.
[16] *M.c.* 13.18 ff. Quotation: Tit 3:2.
[17] *Sk.* 8.
[18] *Ibid.* 9.
[19] *Ibid.* 10.
[20] *Pr.* 93.
[21] *KG* V.47.
[22] *Ibid.* IV.59.

The struggle against the demons and their tempting thoughts, how-ever, is only the negative aspect of irascibility's "natural" working. At the outset, it was said that its task consisted of "struggling for virtue."[23] Accordingly, Evagrius continues: "It is anger's nature ... to fight against every kind of pleasure."[24] For man is designed for both bliss (μακαριότης) and "pleasure" (ἡδονή). Yet like all things, this openness or "receptivity" can be perverted, as Evagrius says.

> And so the angels, on the one hand, suggest to us spiritual pleasure and the blessedness that will come from it [as true knowledge alone can effect this], and they urge us to turn our irascibility against the demons. These latter, on the other hand, drag us toward worldly desires and compel the irascible part, contrary to its nature, to fight with people, so that, with the mind darkened and fallen from knowl-edge, it may become the traitor of the virtues.[25]

Here it already becomes clear that the battle against the move-ments of irascibility cannot be limited to a purely negative defensive stance. On the contrary, whoever is angry will have to do everything in his might in a positive sense in order to restore the "soul's irascible part" to its "operation in accordance with nature." Accordingly, the most important remedy for an inflamed irascibility is the virtue that is its exact opposite: spiritual love in all its various manifestations.[26]

*

In the following scholastic "definition," such as Evagrius liked so well, an attempt is made to define more closely the impulses of "wrath" (ὀργή) and "anger" (θυμός) and to demarcate them from each other. Here Evagrius, as is often the case, follows Clement of Alexandria and in addition to him, the philosophy of his time.

---

[23] *Pr.* 86.
[24] *Ibid.* 24.
[25] *Ibid.* 24.
[26] See Chapter 8.

Stay away from wrath and desist from anger: Wrath is a thirst for vengeance, but revenge is requital for evil.[27] Anger is an assault of the desire of the peaceful soul, [which] above all [plots] revenge.[28]

Evagrius also takes up and further develops the following description of anger having philosophical roots (Aristotelian and Stoic), which allows the perversion of anger's militant nature to be clearly recognized.

Anger is a passion that arises very quickly. Indeed, it is referred to as a boiling over of the irascible part and a movement directed against whoever has committed an injury or is thought to have done so. It renders the soul furious all day long, but especially during prayers, it seizes the mind and portrays to it the face of whoever has hurt it.[29]

An actual or alleged instance of misconduct on the part of our neighbor[30] also brings our irascibility "to a boil," and the soul loses her natural "peacefulness." A wild desire for revenge spreads, which now seeks to reward evil with evil—something strictly forbidden to the Christian.[31] The exceedingly violent and "abrupt" movement, which attacks the soul like a wild animal, makes her "savage" (literally, "bestial" [ἐξαγριοῖ]), as Evagrius often says, meaning it in no wise only figuratively.

Wrath is a senseless passion, and it easily renders frantic those who possess knowledge. It makes the soul bestial and causes her to withdraw from any company.[32] A wrathful monk is a lonely "wild pig." Hardly has he looked at someone, he already snarls.[33] A lion in a

---

[27] *In Ps.* 36:8 ς; cf. Clement of Alexandria, *Stromata* IV.23, 152.

[28] *In Ps.* 36:8 ζ (= *In Ps.* 6:2 α); cf. *Stromata* V.27.10: "For anger is invented as the desirous yearning of an otherwise meek soul, since [anger] desires above all vengeance in an irrational way." Cf. also the commentary by Alain le Boulluec, *Clément d'Alexandrie. Les Stromates. Stromates V. Sources chrétiennes* (*SC*) 279 (Paris: 1981): 120 ff.

[29] Cf. *Pr.* 11.

[30] Cf. *Ant.* V.18, where it is an animal.

[31] Rom 12:17; cf. *Ant.* V.42.

[32] *O. Sp.* 4.1.

[33] *Ibid.* 4.

cage constantly flexes his spine, and the angry man in his cell stirs thoughts of anger.[34]

As we saw in chapter two, what is meant in this "becoming bestial" is the change of man into a "demon": for a demon is a being dominated by anger,[35] and the "wild beasts of the field" are its biblical symbol.[36] Consequently, when Evagrius says that anger "makes a soul bestial,"[37] he means by this that the soul itself, through its behavior, becomes a "demon,"[38] a "basilisk."[39] Likewise, that "wild pig" that destroys "the vineyard" of the soul is nothing else but a biblical symbol of Satan.[40]

Coming quite suddenly to a boil, wrath and anger are frequently quite short-lived. If this vice is not healed, however, this momentary impulse easily turns into resentment, literally the "remembrance of evil" (μνησικακία), and sheer "hatred" (μῖσος). We will meet these "thoughts" when we look into the consequences of the vice of anger.

*

We have already said that the "bodily passions" are relatively short-lived, whereas those of the soul—and this point applies particularly to envy and resentment—"last into old age."[41] What is more, sins of anger are even characteristic of old age! "Caution the old people against anger, but warn the young to rule their stomach. The mental demons wage war against the former; the bodily demons mostly against the latter."[42]

The "mental demons" are naturally those that stir up the passions of the soul, while the "bodily" ones are those that arouse the passions of the body. The demons have, so to speak, different domains of activ-

---

[34] *Ibid.* 7.
[35] *KG* I.68.
[36] *In Ps.* 73:19 θ.
[37] *Ibid.* 57:5 β.
[38] *KG* III.76.
[39] *Ep.* 56.4, 5.
[40] *In Ps.* 79:13 ζ.
[41] *Ep.* 35.3.
[42] *Gn.* 31.

ity.[43] The distinction between "young" and "old" is not, as one might hastily think, merely a question of physical ages and their differing needs. The "young" (νέοι) are more like beginners in the spiritual life; the "old" (γέροντες), by contrast, are the advanced or even the perfect. The "days" in which they—like Abraham[44]—are rich (or ought to be) symbolize "knowledge."[45] Consequently, the "old ones" are the contemplatives: the ones whom the demon of anger primarily importunes, since nothing disturbs the intellect so much, and thereby destroys contemplation, as anger, resentment, and the like. From this point of view, the roles alternate in turn.

> A meek youth endures much, but who will tolerate a fainthearted old man? I saw an irate old man who was exalted because of his age, but greater hope had one younger than he.[46]

For meekness is indeed "the mother of knowledge."[47] The outstanding virtue of the contemplative is then also—seen negatively—his angerlessness (ἀοργησία),[48] or from the positive point of view, his meekness, as we shall see more precisely later on. Both virtues play a key role in the spiritual life.

"Prayer is an offspring of meekness and angerlessness."[49] It is no wonder then that the demons try their best to destroy "this peaceful condition of the rational soul."[50] They know very well that "no virtue fosters wisdom as much as meekness."[51] Accordingly, this is the target of the demons' attacks.

> Stop the mouths of those who in your earshot speak evil [of others], and do not be surprised when you [yourself] are reprimanded by the crowd; this is indeed a temptation on the part of the demons. The

---

[43]Cf. *In Ps.* 117:10 β.
[44]Gen 25:8.
[45]*In Ps.* 117:24 ζ; *In Prov.* 10:27 (G.122).
[46]*Mn.* 112.
[47]*Ep.* 27.2.
[48]*Gn.* 4.45; *In Ps.* 131:1 α.
[49]Cf. *Or.* 14.
[50]*Sk.* 3.
[51]*Ep.* 36.3 Gr.

gnostic must, of course, be free of hatred and resentment, even when it does not suit them![52]

The "gnostic" mentioned here is the Evagrian "contemplative" (θεωρητικός), a person who not only speaks about God, but also "knows"[53] him from within a heartfelt intimacy[54] and who "was made worthy of knowledge" by him.[55]

---

[52]*Gn.* 32.

[53]*Mn.* 120; cf. *Or.* 61.

[54]*KG* V.26.

[55]Thus even in the title of the *Gnostikos* and stereotypically in the *Scholia on the Psalms*, etc.

CHAPTER 5

The Consequences

Hardly anyone will doubt that anger, wrath, and resentment have consequences not only for interpersonal relationships but also for our neighbor himself. Yet few are aware that they cause the greatest damage to themselves as a result of these passions.

> Wrath: robbery of prudence,
> collapse of the [inner] condition,
> confusion of nature,
> wild appearance,
> smelting furnace of the heart,
> flame bursting forth,
> law of irascibility,
> grudge over insults,
> mother of wild beasts,
> silent struggle,
> hindrance to prayer.[1]

In the next chapter we will investigate in detail the consequences for the prayer mentioned here at the end. But first, our discussion ought to concern only specific consequences in the domain of the psyche, the irrational part of the soul. As we have already seen, Evagrius defines wrath as the "boiling of irascibility."[2] The result is the confusion or troubling (ταράσσειν) of the intellect,[3] a condition diametrically opposed to meekness. Evagrius defines meekness as the

---

[1] *Life of Evagrius* (*Vita*) (PG 79.1144A).
[2] *Pr.* 11.
[3] *In Ps.* 6:8 δ; 30:10 δ et passim.

"imperturbability (ἀταραξία) of the irascible power."[4] Yet this imperturbability, especially when everything assaults a person, is an indispensable prerequisite for prayer.[5] Again, this makes it understandable why demons do their utmost to "disturb" such steadfastness. On the psychological level, this inward agitation results in a symptom Evagrius mentions quite often: frightful nightmares.

> "Let not the sun go down upon your wrath,"[6] lest the demons approach you [unexpectedly] sometime during the night and frighten the soul and [thus] make the intellect fearful of the fight on the next day. For the frightful apparitions have the habit of arising from the agitation of anger, and nothing turns the intellect more into a deserter than an irritated irascibility.[7]

The things that happen to us in sleep are for Evagrius "the psychologist" naturally of the greatest significance. In contrast with his time, he was interested in dreams not as harbingers of future events, but as revealers of our present spiritual condition. Evagrius knows that our "dream images" (φαντασίαι) have several causes. "Some spring from the rational part of the soul, when the memory is stimulated; others from the irascible part; others again from the desiring part."[8] In order to see more clearly into this, Evagrius devotes several chapters of his *Praktikos* to those things "which occur in sleep."[9] Characteristic of an aroused irascibility are fear-inducing nightmares:

> Then there comes a time when [wrath] persists longer, is transformed into indignation, [and] stirs up alarming experiences by night. This is succeeded by a general debility of the body, malnutrition with its attendant pallor, and the illusion of being attacked by poisonous wild beasts. These four last mentioned consequences following upon indignation may be found to accompany many [other] thoughts.[10]

---

[4]*In Ps.* 131:1 α.
[5]*Or.* 21, 68, 82, 89, 109.
[6]Eph 4:26.
[7]Cf. *Pr.* 21; cf. *In Prov.* 3:24–25 (end of G.36).
[8]*In Ps.* 143:1 α.
[9]*Pr.* 54–56.
[10]*Pr.* 11.

Indeed, Evagrius reports similar things arising from grief[11] and pride,[12] often returning to this theme, which apparently was very important to him. His (to some extent) quite detailed descriptions are evidence of his own experience and of experiences other anchorites disclosed to him. Particularly in his *Antirrhētikos*, Evagrius frequently related phenomena he had seen with his own eyes,[13] either personally experienced or witnessed by him. From Palladius we know that he was regularly visited by many who sought advice.[14]

Upon reading the different descriptions of these nightmares in context, well-defined common traits become apparent. The texts frequently refer to wild, often venomous animals repeatedly mentioned in the fourth chapter of the *Antirrhētikos*, "On Grief." It remains to modern psychologists to research this in greater detail.

> Employ[ing] for this combat phantasms . . . the demons stimulate the irascible appetite [and] constrain us to walk along precipitous paths where they have us encounter armed men, poisonous snakes and man-eating beasts. We are filled with terror before such sights, and fleeing we are pursued by the beasts and the armed men.[15]

Other texts mention that the anchorites "at night during sleep fight against winged asps, are surrounded by rapacious beasts, encircled by serpents, and cast down from high mountains."[16] Again and again, we are assured that "it is above all those who are wrathful and angry among the brothers whom such frightening visions befall."[17]

> The angry man beholds confusing dreams, and the wrathful man imagines the assault of wild beasts.[18]

*

---

[11]*Ant.* IV.8, 11, 18, 22, etc.
[12]*M.c.* 21.23 ff., 23.13 ff.; *Mn.* 62; *O. Sp.* 8.9.
[13]E.g. *Ant.* IV.36, 72.
[14]*Vita E.*
[15]*Pr.* 54.
[16]*M.c.* 27.1–5.
[17]*Ibid.* 19 f.
[18]*O. Sp.* 4.20.

In his writings, Evagrius speaks almost without exception to monks, and here again primarily to anchorites, i.e. monks who, like himself, lived a purely contemplative life in great solitude. In this context, interpersonal contacts are not at all excluded, but relatively seldom. For this reason, they are not in the least regarded lightly, but rather hold greater meaning for the anchorite because they are lived out and experienced more consciously and intensively. Thus, special conditions had to be fulfilled for withdrawal not only from the world but also from the monastic community itself. Whoever did not keep the corresponding rules but acted out of self-will would destroy the fruits of his effort, since his unresolved problems (namely those developing from living in community) would unfailingly beset him in solitude, wreaking revenge through the nightly terrors here mentioned. In short, whoever did not get along well with others in community would also not get along well with himself in isolation. Thus, one can say proverbially: "Better the thousandth one [in the monastery] with love, than alone with hatred in inaccessible caves."[19]

Not by chance does Evagrius make the "monks who live in cenobia or [small] communities," and perhaps are looking for the supposed silence of a cell in the desert, take note of this warning. In the same text, we also read: "Withdrawal in love purifies the heart, but withdrawal with hate bewilders it."[20]

It is no accident that the first aphorism is a quotation from a writing by Pachomius,[21] who himself began as an anchorite and went on to become the father of a community of monks numbering in the thousands. Evagrius does not cite him on account of himself being critical of the eremitic life; rather, for him it is a matter of protecting this form of life from abuse. The following definition gives us a first hint as to wherein the positive meaning of this withdrawal to the

---

[19] *Mn.* 9.

[20] *Ibid.* 8.

[21] Cf. L. Théophile Lefort, "À propos d'un aphorisme d'Evagrius Ponticus." *Bulletin de l'Académie Royale de Belgique. Classe des lettres et des sciences morales et politiques,* 5e série 36 (1950): 70–79.

wilderness lies for him. "An anchorite is one who lives a devout and upright life in the world that exists in his mind."[22]

As the Apostle says, all Christians should "live sober, upright, and godly lives in this world," but in order to do so, they must first "renounce irreligion and worldly passions,"[23] which material things may awaken in us when our soul is not one with itself. By contrast, the anchorite is a person who not only lives uprightly and piously in the outer world, but also in its spiritual image, i.e. in that inner cosmos that emerges in our spirit from the various mental images that material reality leaves behind in the form of "copies" or "impressions." The external withdrawal or detachment from worldly occupations is ultimately only a remedy aimed at acquiring this internal detachment.

> To separate the body from the soul is the privilege only of the One who has joined them together. But to separate the soul from the body lies as well in the power of the man who pursues virtue. For our Fathers gave to the meditation of death and to the flight from the body a special name: *anachōrēsis* [withdrawal].[24]

"To separate the soul from the body" means nothing other than to free her from the tyranny of the passions so as to let virtue live. But the passions of the soul follow us up until physical death.[25] Under such conditions, premature withdrawal is not without harm, particularly if one has neglected to come to terms with one's fellow human beings. Interpersonal relationships offer demons their main field of attack for those living in community.[26]

> Let no anchorite embrace the solitary life under the influence of anger, pride or sadness, nor let him flee from the brothers while being troubled by these thoughts. [For to depart into the desert in this condition would mean running aground on the demons' mali-

---

[22] *Sk.* 14.
[23] Tit 2:12.
[24] *Pr.* 52.
[25] *Ibid.* 36.
[26] *Ibid.* 5; cf. 48.

cious cunning.][27] From the passions mentioned, there especially arise states of distraction (ἐκστάσεις) of the heart, which then moves from one thought to another and from this one to a fourth one and so, step by step, sinks into the abyss of oblivion.[28]

Thoughts of anger also easily arise from such thoughts of pride, as we have already seen.[29] The continuation of the cited text also indicates this:

This passion most often befalls one through thoughts of pride. When someone embraces the solitary life in such a state, he sees the air of his cell all on fire, and during the night, [beholds] lightning that shines on the walls. Next [come] the voices of pursuers and those pursued, chariots that appear in the air, and [he sees] the entire house filled with Ethiopians[30] and terror. On account of his overwhelming cowardice, he sinks into folly, becomes dizzy, and in his anxiety forgets his human condition . . .[31]

Although a modern reader may find much in this description that appears truly picturesque, it is nonetheless an important observation that disturbed human relationships, such as those wrought by wrath, pride, or also grief (and the depressions linked to these), have the worst consequences for the afflicted person when he finds himself alone. Naturally, these connections are well known to the demons from experience, and as a result they advance strategically, having previously driven us into these passions.

When, having seized on a pretext, the irascible part of our soul is troubled, then at the same moment the demons suggest to us that *anachōrēsis* is a fine thing, lest we resolve the causes of our sadness and free ourselves from the disturbance.[32]

---

[27] *Ibid.* 22.
[28] *M.c.* 23.1–7.
[29] *Pr.* 14.
[30] In the literature of the early monks, demons often appear as "Ethiopians," i.e. black people.
[31] *M.c.* 23.13–22.
[32] Cf. *Pr.* 22.

*

If we reflect for a moment, we notice that the consequences of an unconquered outbreak of anger stand in a paradoxical relationship to the outbreak itself. If the brute behaves like a roaring "lion"[33] or an aggressive "lonely wild pig,"[34] running around "with bloodshot eyes,"[35] at night he turns into a being that is terrorized by fearful and nightmarish states. Evagrius speaks similarly of the consequences of pride,[36] which is closely linked to anger. Examined in detail, however, this paradox is entirely explainable: for while the one dominated by anger turns into a "demon" at day,[37] at night he is tormented by the very same demons. The one who strives after the spiritual life should be on guard against anger! The following text may serve us as a transition to the next chapter.

> The one who strives for pure prayer and wishes to lead his intellect to God without thoughts should master anger and be on guard against the thoughts arising from this. I mean, the thoughts that befall us out of mistrust, hatred, and resentment, which most often blind the intellect and ruin its heavenly condition. St. Paul also advised us thus, saying that one "should pray, lifting holy hands without anger or quarreling."[38]
>
> Of course, a bad habit has followed the monks [into the desert]; and they often bring suit against family members and quarrel over money that is owed or goods for the relief of the poor. As we have said, these are mocked by the demons and make the path of monastic life harder for themselves by stirring up anger on account of money, and then by means of money hasten to extinguish [this anger]. It is as though one put out his eyes in order to put a salve on them. For the Lord has charged us to sell our possessions and give

---

[33] *O. Sp.* 4.7.
[34] *Ibid.* 4.4.
[35] *Ibid.* 10.
[36] *Ibid.* 8.9.
[37] *Pr.* 21 ff.
[38] I Tim 2:8.

[the proceeds] to the poor,[39] but not with strife and lawsuit! For "the Lord's servant must not be quarrelsome,"[40] but "if any one strikes you on the right cheek, turn to him the other also; and if anyone would sue you and take your coat, let him have your cloak as well."[41] Likewise, in the future he should take great pains that he not only not go on as one who earns, but also that he not die as one who was slain by the thought of resentment, inasmuch as "the ways of the vengeful lead to death," according to Solomon the wise.[42]

Moreover, every man who withholds such riches should know that he has robbed the blind, the lame, and the lepers of their livelihood and shelter, and that he will have to render an account on the Day of Judgment.[43]

---

[39]Matt 19:21.
[40]2 Tim 2:24.
[41]Matt 5:39 f.
[42]Prov 12:28.
[43]*M.c.* 32.26 ff.

Anger and Prayer

From everything that we have heard up to now, it is clear that anger is an odious vice. It "animalizes" man and turns him into a "demon." Furthermore, whoever allows himself to be dominated by this vice becomes a plaything of the demons, who terrorize such a bold person through frightful nocturnal visions. Had Evagrius nothing more to say on this subject, studying his writings would hardly be worthwhile. But we stand only at the beginning!

> The man who stores up [grounds for] injuries and resentments and yet fancies that he prays might as well draw water from a well and pour it into a cask that is full of holes.[1]

The surpassing importance Evagrius ascribes to anger in all his writings is based on its utterly negative relation to prayer, as several preceding texts have already indicated. "Prayer" is understood here as the quintessence of the spiritual life or of "mysticism," as we say today.

> Every war fought between us and the impure spirits is engaged in for no other cause than that of spiritual prayer. This is an activity that is intolerable to them; they find it hostile and oppressive. To us, on the other hand, it is both pleasant in its highest degree and spiritually profitable.[2]

In support of his strong conviction that anger and prayer—like fire and water—are mutually exclusive, Evagrius can appeal not only to Holy Scripture, but also to the "hidden and ancient custom of people":

---

[1]*Or.* 22.
[2]*Or.* 49.

59

Tell me, why do you plunge into battle so quickly if you have renounced food, honor, and possessions? Why do you feed the dog [i.e., anger] if you profess to possess nothing? When it barks and attacks people, it is clear that it has something in the house and wants to keep it. Such a [man], I am convinced, is far from pure prayer, for I know that anger destroys such prayer.

Moreover, I am surprised that he has even forgotten the saints: David, who exhorts us, "Refrain from anger, and forsake wrath!"[3]; and Ecclesiastes, who urges us, "Remove anger from your heart, and put away evil from your flesh"[4]; while the Apostle commands that always and everywhere, men should "lift holy hands [to the Lord] without anger or quarreling."[5]

And why do we not learn from the hidden and ancient custom of people driving dogs out of the house during prayer? This indicates allegorically that those who pray should be free from anger. And further, "the anger of dragons is their wine."[6] But Nazirites (i.e., those consecrated to God) are to abstain from wine.[7]

The gall bladder and the haunch were inedible for the gods, as one of the wise pagans unwittingly said, I surmise. I mean that the first is a symbol of anger, while the second is that of irrational desire.[8]

*

The negative effects of an inflamed irascibility on the one who prays are at first glance once again of a purely psychological nature.

All demonic thoughts introduce into the soul mental representations of sensory objects, and the intellect, marked by them, then carries the forms of these objects around with itself. The approaching demon is then recognized by means of the objects themselves.

---

[3]Ps 36:8.
[4]Eccl 11:10.
[5]1 Tim 2:8.
[6]Deut 32:33.
[7]Num 6:3.
[8]*M.c.* 5.12–34.

For example, if the face of one who has done me some harm or has dishonored me arises in my mind, then the approaching thought of resentment is thus transferred.[9]

Thus it is with reason that the Holy Spirit convicts us: "You sit and speak against your brother; you slander your own mother's son."[10] You have opened the door to thoughts of resentment and have confused the intellect at the time of prayer by constantly imagining the face of your enemy and by making him into a "God," for what the intellect sees when it prays can justly be called a "God."[11]

Evagrius describes here an experience which no doubt everyone has had once: the almost obsessive fixation on an object—or worse, on a particular person who has actually or allegedly insulted us and away from whom one cannot tear one's thoughts precisely during prayer. Under such circumstances, prayer becomes a caricature; we will return to this point.

*

How do the demons actually know by which passion we are being assailed at any given moment? Evagrius spoke of mere "mental images" (νοήματα) that the demons supply to us. The demons do not know our "heart," that is, our intellect or inmost being; this statement is of great significance for Evagrius. This inner sanctum is inaccessible to them. Only God, who has created it, knows our heart.[12] Still, the demons are first-rate, experienced observers of our behavior on account of their long presence in creation: even the smallest and to us completely unconscious movement does not elude them.[13] From these "signs" (σύμβολα) they recognize what is hidden in our hearts, from whence proceed our good or evil intentions. From these treacherous signs, they create the material of their temptations[14] by stimu-

---

[9]*Ibid.* 2.1–7.
[10]Ps 49:20.
[11]*M.c.* 37.19–25.
[12]*Ibid.* 1 ff.; reference to Ps 32:15 and Acts 1:24.
[13]*Ep.* 16.
[14]*M.c.* 37.4 ff.

lating, for example, our memory during prayer[15] and furnishing us with the image of the one who has offended us. We then hold this image before our eyes like an "idol" in order to converse with it instead of with God.[16]

All material things make an "imprint" on our mind, of course; that is, they leave behind in it an "image" (εἴδολον)[17] or an impression (τύπος),[18] which we mentally regard as though it were the actual object itself. Only God, who is altogether "immaterial"[19] and "formless"[20] (since he is "bodiless") leaves the intellect—in person or also in the guise of his "thought"— "without impress."[21] He is "without intermediary" (μηδενὸς μεσιτεύοντος)[22]—personal, we would say—present, and accordingly also working without an intermediary.[23]

Now, if we have a falling out with a fellow human being—whether we are the cause or not—and have "passionately" reacted to this incident, then, as a demonic thought, the "image" (εἰκών) of a perceptible human being is imprinted in our mind, with which we then "speak or interact secretly in a lawless way,"[24] as though the corresponding person were present. This converse with images has catastrophic effects above all "at the time of prayer," when the intellect should be "free of images" precisely because it is then holding converse with the immaterial and formless God.

Whoever "desires to pray 'as we ought'[25] and grieves someone 'runs in vain.'"[26] His supposed prayer is nothing else but a "mimicry" (ἀνατύπωσις) of reality that now provokes God's anger.[27] Hence the warning:

---

[15]Or. 45–47.
[16]M.c. 37.24.
[17]Ibid. 4.16.
[18]M.c. 41.1 ff.
[19]Or. 67.
[20]Ibid.
[21]In Ps. 140:2 α.
[22]Or. 3.
[23]Cf. ibid. 64.
[24]Sk. 13.
[25]Rom 8:26.
[26]Or. 20.
[27]Ibid. 145, 146.

Whatever you might do by way of avenging yourself on a brother who has done you some injustice will turn into a stumbling block for you at the time of prayer.[28]

The same, of course, is also true for the brother whom we have offended and to whom we have not then been reconciled.

Be very attentive lest ever you cause some brother to become a fugitive through your anger. For if this should happen, your whole life long you will yourself not be able to flee from the demon of sadness. At the time of prayer this will be a constant stumbling block to you.[29]

With full justification one can say then that in prayer, a type of "tribunal" on our inner condition is held.[30]

When you find yourself tempted or contradicted; or when you get irritated or when you grow angry through encountering some opposition or feel the urge to utter some kind of invective—then is the time to put yourself in mind of prayer and of the judgment to be passed on such doings. You will find that the disordered movement will immediately be stilled.[31]

Do not give yourself over to your angry thoughts so as to fight in your mind with the one who has vexed you. Nor again to thoughts of fornication, imagining the pleasure vividly. The one darkens the soul; the other invites to the burning of passion. Both cause your mind to be defiled and while you indulge these fancies at the time of prayer, and thus do not offer pure prayer to God, the demon of acedia falls upon you without delay. He falls above all upon souls in this state and, dog-like, snatches away the soul as if it were a fawn.[32]

Once more, this text discloses quite beautifully how the various "thoughts" arise from one another. The one who is to blame for an

---

[28]*Ibid.* 13.
[29]*Pr.* 25.
[30]Cf. *Ep.* 25.6.
[31]*Or.* 12.
[32]*Pr.* 23.

enduring estrangement from a fellow brother no longer escapes from the demon of sadness during his lifetime because he cannot possibly undo what has happened. The pangs of conscience that arise sooner or later remain fruitless. But sadness is the twin brother of boredom, which at the time of prayer plunges us into this peculiar condition of acedia (soul-weariness), which Evagrius has so aptly described.[33]

*

The goal of the practical life (πρακτική) is to bring as an offering to God a prayer that is "pure" of all passionate "thoughts" and "images" and finally, in general, of mental representations of created things.[34] This also means that nothing distracts or "scatters" our intellect. Such "undistracted prayer" is a great thing[35]; indeed, it is the "highest act of the intellect."[36] One can also say—in an Evagrian sense—that man is fully himself only in prayer, since in this immediate and personal "intercourse of the spirit with God,"[37] the created "image" finds its way back to the uncreated "archetype" which is its end goal.[38] Satan, who disturbed this relationship already at the beginning,[39] does not cease even now to frustrate this dialogue in every conceivable way.

> When the spirit begins to be free from all distractions as it makes its prayer, then there commences an all-out battle day and night against the irascible part.[40]

It would be an error to think that this struggle diminishes to the extent that one makes progress in the spiritual life. The opposite is

---

[33] Cf. G. Bunge, *Akedia. Die geistliche Lehre des Evagrios Pontikos vom Überdruß* (Würzburg: Der christliche Osten, 1995⁴).

[34] *Or.* 56–58.

[35] *Pr.* 69.

[36] *Or.* 34.

[37] *Ibid.* 3.

[38] In his *Letter to Melania*, Evagrius developed an entire theory of the direct knowledge of God from the relationship between the original image (*Urbild*) and what is formed according to its likeness (*Abbild*)!

[39] Cf. Gen 3.

[40] *Pr.* 63.

the case! The demon of anger attacks most fiercely[41] not the beginners, but the "elders" in knowledge, that is, the "spiritual fathers" who
"have already received the gift of the Spirit."[42] For with the "contemplatives," the "ones who see," the sins of anger have the most devas-
tating consequences: they blind the intellect's "eyes," with which it
beholds God and perceives his creation.

> By night the demons demand the spiritual master for themselves—
> to harass him. By day they surround him with pressures from men—
> with calumnies and with dangers.[43]

Accordingly, Evagrius forcefully warns those who "are still held by
sin and still subject to fits of anger" not to "strive shamelessly after
knowledge of more divine things or to rise up to the level of immaterial prayer."[44] Their supposed "prayer in spirit and in truth" would
then be, of course, nothing but a grotesque caricature of "true prayer."
God would not leave such an outrage unpunished.

> Just as it hardly is of benefit to a man with bad eyes to stand gazing
> at the midday sun, when it is hottest, with fixed attention and uncov-
> ered eyes, so also is it of no avail at all for an impure spirit, still sub-
> ject to passions, to counterfeit that awesome and surpassing prayer
> in spirit and truth. On the contrary, it stirs up the resentment of God
> against itself.[45]

Evagrius then was already well aware of what we today call "self-
induced states," which one only "spuriously" feels without actually
experiencing them. It is significant that primarily those who "are still
held by sin and still subject to fits of anger" incline to such "imita-
tions" (ἀνατυπώσεις). It is pride, hiding behind this anger, that drives
them not to wait to be called (as was Moses by God from the Burning Bush)[46] but rather daringly to set foot in "the place of prayer."

[41]*Gn.* 31.
[42]*Ep.* 52.7.
[43]*Or.* 139.
[44]*Ibid.* 145.
[45]*Ibid.* 146.
[46]*M.c.* 17.36 ff.; cf. *Or.* 4.

"True prayer" is indeed a "bestowal of grace" (χάρισμα),[47] a gift (δῶρον)[48] God gives "to the man who prays"[49] and of which one must be "deemed worthy."[50] So should the one inflamed with anger not pray at all? By no means! But instead of reaching for what is unattainable and even dangerous on account of his passionate condition, he should resort to those "short and intense"[51] invocations of Christ, mentioned everywhere in the early monastic literature: those "short prayers" (as Augustine calls them), out of which the well-known "Jesus Prayer" developed.[52]

If you want to put the enemy to flight, pray without ceasing.[53]

These "concise," "terse," "repeated," indeed "ceaseless" short prayers are the daily bread of whoever is tempted—even of him who is tempted directly by the demon of anger.[54] They are offered with tears, because nothing better softens "the inherent crudeness of the soul"[55]—which is indeed of demonic origin.[56] But on this point, we have already arrived at the remedies for the inflamed irascibility, which we will later discuss at length.[57]

---

[47]*Or.* 87.

[48]*Ibid.* 69.

[49]*Ibid.* 58.

[50]*In Ps.* 13:7 ζ, 43:4 γ, etc.

[51]*Or.* 98.

[52]Cf. G. Bunge, *Earthen Vessels: The Practice of Personal Prayer According to the Patristic Tradition* (San Francisco: Ignatius Press, 2002).

[53]*In Ps.* 55:10 ε. Quotation: 1 Thes 5:17.

[54]*Pr.* 54.

[55]Cf. *Or.* 5.

[56]Cf. *ibid.* 91; *Pr.* 50 et passim.

[57]See under chapter 8.

CHAPTER 7

The Blinding of the Intellect

T he expression "blind wrath" is likely known to all: for example, we speak of someone pouncing on another person or thing "in a blind wrath." What is mostly meant by this is that a man, in his agitation, loses his ability to see to a certain extent. Nonetheless, Evagrius has a more profound understanding of this "blindness."

> Remove the thoughts of anger
> from your soul,
> and let anger not abide
> in your heart,
> and you will never be bewildered
> at the time of prayer.
> For as the smoke of chaff troubles the eyes,
> so does resentment trouble the intellect
> at the time of prayer.[1]

Resentment confuses and "troubles" (ταράσσει) the "intelligible eye"[2] of the soul, the intellect; worse still, an agitated irascibility "blinds the seer" (τὸν ὁρῶντα).[3] In short, "nothing darkens"[4] and "so blinds the intellect like an agitated anger."[5] The image of the "eye" is not just a metaphor: for as the body has five senses, so too does the intellect have five spiritual senses. And just as the bodily organ of sight perceives material things directly, so too does the spiritual organ

---

[1]*O. Sp.* 4.16.
[2]Cf. *Or.* 27.
[3]*KG* V.27.
[4]*In Ps.* 30:10 ζ.
[5]*Ibid.* 6:8 δ.

of sight lay bare to the intellect the intelligible things as they are (ψιλά).[6] And just as our bodily organ of sight is made manifest through our bodily eyes, so too does the intellect have two "intelligible eyes" through which it "beholds" (that is, recognizes)[7] God, be it either indirectly through the "reasons" of created natures or "unmediatedly" and personally "at the time of prayer." But an excited anger destroys this twofold perception.

> The demonic thoughts blind the soul's left eye, which is devoted to the contemplation of creation, while mental representations that imprint and shape our intellect (ἡγεμονικόν) darken the right eye, which at the time of prayer beholds the blessed light of the Holy Trinity. It is through this eye also that the bride in the Song of Songs[8] delighted the heart of the Bridegroom himself.[9]

For now, our interest lies only in the beginning of this most mystical text. All "thoughts" (pejoratively speaking) are ultimately of demonic origin. But this holds particularly true, as we have seen, for thoughts of anger. Consequently, if these "blind" the intellect (that is, "the beholder"), then the intellect can no longer recognize "created things" (τὰ γεγονότα) as they really are.[10] The "contemplation of the created" embraces all that God has created, is creating, and will yet create in space and time. It is easy to see what consequences spiritual "blindness" will have here!

*

> Knowledge coming to us from the outside endeavors to show objects through their reasons [λόγοι], while that [knowledge] that is imparted to us by the grace of God places things directly before the eyes (αὐτοψεί) of the mind; and the intellect, in considering them, allows their reasons to draw nigh to it. Error is opposed to the first

---

[6] *KG* II.35.
[7] Cf. *ibid.* V.54, 57 etc.
[8] Song 4:9.
[9] *M.c.* 42.
[10] Cf. *KG* VI.63.

[knowledge], while wrath and anger and what follows from these is opposed to the second.[11]

While the "knowledge which comes from men is strengthened by careful meditation and diligent exercise," the knowledge "that by God's grace has come to be within us" requires the virtues of justice, angerlessness, and compassion. "The first [knowledge] can be received by those still subject to passion; the second [knowledge] is received only by those [who have obtained] passionlessness (ἀπάθεια)—those who are also able at the time of prayer to contemplate the illuminating gentle radiance (φέγγος) proper to their intellect (νοῦς)." Thus Evagrius heard from the mouth of his teacher Basil, "the pillar of truth."[12]

The "external wisdom," that of the "wise of this world,"[13] is only a question of intellectual accomplishment. Its preferred means, next to study and practice, is "dialectic."[14] An error (πλάνη) in this domain is, so to speak, only a "technical failure," which as such does not bring discredit to the "scientist" and likewise can hardly be imputed to him as a moral failure.

Standing in complete contrast to this is the knowledge that flows toward us "from God" (ἐκ θεοῦ), "from God's grace" (ἐκ θεοῦ χάριτος)—to become a partaker of which intellectual accomplishments do not suffice.

The knowledge of Christ requires not a soul [skilled in] dialectic, but one that sees: for while impure souls may become dialecticians, seeing is reserved for the pure.[15]

"Purity" means "passionlessness": above all, freedom from "wrath, resentment and what follows these," such as envy, suspicions, resentment, and the like. In a positive sense, the "seeing one" requires most of all the virtue of justice, which "is located in the whole of the soul,"

---

[11] *Gn.* 4.
[12] *Ibid.* 45.
[13] *KG* I.73; VI.22.
[14] *Ibid.* IV.90.
[15] *Ibid.* Gr.

common to all three powers, and whose work is to bring about "a certain harmony and symphony among the various parts of the soul."[16] This virtue of justice was emphasized not only by Gregory of Nazianzus,[17] to whom Evagrius owes so much, but also by Antony the Great, whom he significantly portrays as a great contemplative.

> A certain member of what was then considered the circle of the wise once approached the just Antony and asked him: "How do you ever manage to carry on, Father, deprived as you are of the consolation of books?" His reply: "My book, sir philosopher, is the nature of created things, and it is always at hand when I wish to read [in it] the words [or reasons (λόγοι)] of God."[18]

After this are required the virtues of angerlessness and compassion. When the gnostic—the contemplative as spiritual master—teaches, he must thus be free of anger, resentment, and sorrow.[19] Angerlessness is even the virtue the gnostic needs most of all.[20]

> Just as a well that has been cleansed of objects that had fallen into it lets clear water flow, so too does the intellect, purified of anger, resentment, and sensual perception, find pure knowledge and gives sweet desire to the one who has acquired these.[21]

The knowledge—passively received[22]—that is bestowed upon the gnostic is not mere learning, but is acquired directly through "one's own eyes" (αὐτοψεί)—a knowledge of things as they really are[23]: namely, as creatures of God, to whom such creatures bear witness in their own way. While "dialectic" necessarily makes use of thoughts (λογισμοί), mental representations (νοήματα) or visual concepts (θεωρήματα) developed from material reality,[24] God works his knowl-

---

[16]Cf. *Pr.* 89.

[17]*Gn.* 44.

[18]*Pr.* 92.

[19]*Gn.* 10.

[20]*Ibid.* 5.

[21]*Institutes to the Monks supplement* (*Inst. mon. suppl.*) 23.

[22]*KG* I.34; cf. *Gn.* 4.

[23]*Gn.* 4.

[24]*In Eccl.* 5:1–2 (G.35).

edge directly in the soul,[25] for which reason the contemplative must also consciously transcend these resources of our understanding[26] if he wants to hold "discourse with God without any intermediary."[27]

*

While an error in the domain of "knowledge that comes to us from without" is only of relative significance, since it can be rectified through careful "study" (for "scientific knowledge" in principle always moves forward despite all temporary mistakes and setbacks), matters in the domain of "knowledge proceeding from God" are altogether different. Here, man's inner condition is of decisive importance, because "like a strong storm, resentment drives the intellect away from this knowledge."[28]

> The temptation of the gnostic is a spurious conjecture, which presents itself to the intellect either as [really] existing, when it does not exist, as not existing when it does exist, or as existing in some manner which it does not. [29]
>
> The sin of the gnostic is false knowledge concerning matters themselves or their contemplations, which is caused by some passion or because this is not in sight of the good that is being [investigatively] discussed.[30]

From such "spurious conjectures" and ultimately "false knowledge," such occurrences arise in the domain of faith, which we commonly call "heresies": "shipwrecks of faith,"[31] which can destroy the eternal salvation of their victims, should the latter not repent of them.

> "War is waged, war with the skill of a pilot": Those who suffer shipwreck with regard to faith do not fight against the spirits opposed to theology with the skill of a pilot. The same can also be

---

[25] *Or.* 65.
[26] *Ibid.* 56–58; *M.c.* 40.
[27] *Or.* 3.
[28] Cf. *Mn.* 13.
[29] *Gn.* 42.
[30] *Ibid.* 43.
[31] 1 Tim 1:19.

said of each virtue. For there is also a shipwreck with regard to prudence, love, and freedom from greed. Likewise, with regard to every teaching of the catholic and apostolic Church, shipwreck can result in similar fashion. But if one must "wage war with the skill of a pilot" against the adversaries, then our life on earth resembles a naval battle.[32]

The demons, then, are opposed not only to the virtues (in that they tempt us to their contrary vices) but also in the domain of theology (θεολογική) to the dogmatic teachings[33] of the "catholic and apostolic Church."

"In this way wherein I have walked they hid for me a snare": Our enemies lay a trap in all the virtues. In courage, they conceal the snares of cowardice; in prudence, those of fornication; and in love, they lay the snares of hatred. Into meekness, they instill arrogance; into compassion, a mercifulness not for God's sake but for the sake of the onlooker; and into fasting, fasting for men's sake. And this concerns practice (πρακτική). And indeed, what must one still say about contemplation [and] how many snares the enemies have laid secretly through heresies against orthodox teachings?[34]

"Heresies" then are therefore not mere "dogmatic errors," comparable to "scientific errors," but rather the work of demons in the heads of those who hatch them or who fall to them.[35] Evagrius assures us that he even experienced this in his own life.[36] Only those whose spirit has been previously "blinded" by the demon of anger and who have incurred the loss of the divine "light" of knowledge are susceptible to such demonic blindings. Whoever has had to suffer such a "defeat" and has not repented will easily become "the lead[er] in false teachings and opinions,"[37] a heresiarch, or a founder of sects. With-

---

[32]*In Prov.* 24:6 (G.266).
[33]Cf. *KG* I.10 et passim.
[34]*In Ps.* 141:4 α.
[35]*Mn.* 123.
[36]*Ibid.* 126; cf. *Vita* 11. See under chapter 12.
[37]*KG* V.38.

out himself being aware of this, he thereby does the work of the demon of anger, who "fights [him] night and day."[38]

*

As we have seen above, "the demonic thought blinds the soul's left eye, which is devoted to the contemplation of the created."[39] The afflicted one then arrives, for example, at a "false knowledge of the things themselves or of their contemplation, which accuses the Creator of being unjust or unwise,"[40] i.e., that the world is not an expression of God's justice and wisdom, but rather that men meet an unjust and ultimately senseless fate. Such notions one finds, for instance, in "what is falsely called knowledge (γνῶσις)"[41] of both old and new making.

Moreover, there are also "theological" heresies in a narrower sense: those that are concerned not only with God's actions, but with God's being itself, in that they deny the consubstantiality of the Holy Spirit, for instance. It becomes clear that this is not a matter of purely academic questions from the fact (which Evagrius emphasizes very clearly) that such a denial removes from baptism every soteriological value[42] and thereby also deprives the spiritual life of its ontological foundation! But we can no longer speak of all these things here.

Nonetheless, Evagrius' notion is still thought provoking: that moral defects, without fail, have consequences in the domain of "knowledge" and "spiritual contemplation"; and conversely, that every kind of "heresy" is not simply an intellectual failure, but a work of the demons in the one whom they have previously "blinded" through the vice of anger. How different church history would look, had all those involved in dogmatic disputes taken greater care to beware the sins of anger!

And not only then, when with supposedly "holy zeal" they took to the field against alleged or actual "false teachings," but also in all

---

[38]Cf. *ibid.* IV.47.
[39]*M.c.* 42.
[40]*In Ps.* 143:7 ε.
[41]1 Tim 6:20.
[42]*In Prov.* 22:28 (G.249 with commentary).

those conflicts that have led to divisions within the Church. Evagrius
is convinced that the schisms of church history as well are nothing
else than the work of demons,[43] and above all the demon of anger. On
the contrary, following the words of the prophet Joel,[44] one ought to
solve such conflicts with militant meekness or gentle firmness.[45] The
spiritual life of the person who does not follow this rule and therefore
pays no heed to love—be such a life otherwise quite ascetic[46]—is
nothing more than pious self-deception.

> For this I know for sure, that those who divide the church of the
> Lord are far removed from pure prayer![47]

Indeed, how could such prayer be "pure" when it is tarnished by
thoughts of anger? Let us call to mind here what we said in the preceding chapter about the relationship between anger and prayer.
Whoever fosters resentment in his heart and imagines that he is praying "might as well draw water from a well and pour it into a cask that
is full of holes."[48] The prayer of an angry man is a subtle form of idolatry, because he has before him in his mind not God, but rather constantly the face of the one at whom he is angry.[49] Things are even
worse when such an enraged person "dares shamelessly to strive after
knowledge of more divine things or to rise up to the level of immaterial prayer."[50] His imagined "prayer in spirit and in truth" is then
nothing but "mimicry," and thus a parody, of the highest level of the
spiritual life, which does not make God well disposed to him in the
least. On the contrary, it provokes him to anger against the foolhardy
one.[51] In God's eyes, he is indeed nothing other than a "demon" in
disguise . . .

---

[43]Cf. *Ep.* 52.5.
[44]Joel 3:11: "Let the meek be a warrior."
[45]*Ep.* 24.2.
[46]*Ibid.* 56.5.
[47]*Ibid.* 52.5.
[48]*Or.* 22.
[49]*M.c.* 37.23 ff.
[50]*Or.* 145.
[51]*Ibid.* 146.

CHAPTER 8

The Means of Healing

Allll vices arise from a misuse of the soul's powers, which in themselves are good. In order to heal these "illnesses" of the soul, one must put into practice the virtue contrary to each respective vice. In the case of disease—of "inflammation," as Evagrius says[1]—within the irascible part, these virtues are "courage and perseverance,"[2] and above all, the specifically Christian "love"[3] which manifests itself concretely as "meekness" and "humility."[4] These tackle the vice at the root, so to speak. In addition, as experience teaches, there is still a great number of other remedies in which the aforesaid virtues are put into practice. Let us begin with these. "The work of courage and patience is to know no fear of enemies and eagerly to endure afflictions."[5]

These "enemies" are the demons, naturally, and not one's fellow human beings. As mentioned above, "anger is given to us so that we might fight against the demons."[6] Since these "opponents" are invisible to us[7] and we perceive their workings, generally speaking, only through the evil "thoughts . . . through which they fight against the soul,"[8] our involvement with them occurs mainly at this level.[9] For this reason, "anger according to nature" comes into play here.

---

[1] *Gn.* 47.
[2] *Pr.* 89.
[3] *KG* I.84; cf. 41 et passim.
[4] *In Prov.* 31:21 (G.377).
[5] *Pr.* 89.
[6] *Ibid.* 24.
[7] *KG* I.22.
[8] *Eul.* 15.
[9] *Ant.* Prologue (9).

The boiling of anger, aroused against the demon, is also extremely helpful against such thoughts because he fears above all this anger that is aroused on account of the thoughts and which destroys his mental representations. This is also the meaning of the words: "Be angry but sin not."[10] This cure is useful when administered for such temptations of the soul.[11]

*

This applies to the practical life (πρακτική). In the spiritual life of the "gnostic"—the contemplative—courage has as its task the "steadfast perseverance in the truth, even to the point of combat, as well as refraining from entry into that which has no existence," as Evagrius learned from his teacher, Gregory of Nazianzus.[12] Evagrius explains in detail what role anger is to play in this fight in the following beautiful chapter, the biblical symbolic language of which is no longer transparent without assistance for the modern reader no longer conversant in patristic allegory.

As sheep to a good shepherd, God has given to man mental representations of this world. For as it is written, "He has put eternity into man's heart"[13] by linking it as an aid together with the irascible part and the concupiscible part, so that [man] might through anger chase away the mental representations of the "wolves,"[14] and through desire might lovingly tend the sheep, even if he be struck by frequent downpours and winds. Moreover, he has also given him a "pasture" in order to graze his sheep and a "place of green pasture" and "the water of rest,"[15] a "Psalter" and a "harp,"[16] a "rod" and a "staff,"[17] so

---

[10]Ps 4:5.

[11]*M.c.* 16.16–22. Evagrius is referring here to the temptations of fornication.

[12]*Gn.* 44.

[13]Eccl 3:11; cf. *In Eccl.* 3.10–13 (G.15).

[14]Meant here are the demons; cf. also *M.c.* 13.

[15]Ps 22:2. "As sheep are nourished on grass and water, so too is man enlivened through *praktikē* and knowledge" (*In Ps.* 22:2 α).

[16]Ps 56:11. The Psalter is a symbol of the intellect; the harp represents the soul (*In Ps.* 56:11 ε).

[17]Ps 22:4. The rod symbolizes *praktikē*, while the staff symbolizes knowledge (*In Ps.* 22:4 γ).

that he might feed and clothe himself from this flock and "gather the herbage of the mountains."[18] For it is written, "Who tends a flock without getting some of the milk?"[19]

The anchorite then must keep watch over this flock by day and by night, lest a single one of the mental representations be seized by the "wild animals" or fall into the hands of "robbers." But in case this happens on the valley floor, he must at once deliver it from the mouth of the lion or bear[20] . . .[21]

The "shepherd" whose difficult life Evagrius portrays here is Jacob, the Old Testament model for the *Praktikos*,[22] who after serving seven years for the unloved Leah and then again seven years for the beloved Rachel (symbols of *praktikē* and *gnostikē*[23]) begets "Israel": the contemplative,[24] the "man who sees God."[25]

*

The virtue of courage thus enables irascibility to work in accordance with its nature, that is, "to fight against the demons and strive against every pleasure."[26] Anger, as it were, is the soul's "hound," whose task is to exterminate the "wolves" [i.e., the demons].[27] Consequently, we should direct all our aggressiveness against them.

Hatred against the demons contributes greatly to our salvation and is useful in the working of virtue. Nonetheless, we do not have the power to nurse this hatred within ourselves as a strong sapling

---

[18]Prov 27:25. The "herbage of the mountains" symbolizes the knowledge of God (*In Prov.* 27.25 [G.341]).

[19]1 Cor 9:7.

[20]1 Kg 17:34 f.

[21]*M.c.* 17.1–17.

[22]*In Ps.* 77:21 η; cf. 86:2 α.

[23]*Or.* Prologue.

[24]*In Ps.* 77:21 η.

[25]The meaning of the name "Israel" goes back to Philo of Alexandria (*De Abraham* 57 et passim). Clement of Alexandria took up this meaning, cf. *Pedagogue* I.57.2, 77.2; *Stromata* I.31.4; II.20.2; et passim, and thus transmitted it to Evagrius, an avid reader of Clement.

[26]*Pr.* 24.

[27]*M.c.* 13.18 ff.

because the pleasure-seeking spirits destroy it and invite the soul to return again to friendship and familiar intimacy. This friendship—or rather this cancerous ulcer that is so hard to cure—is healed by the physician of souls through being abandoned [by God]. In particular, he permits us to suffer various terrors by night or by day from [the demons], and the soul hastens back to its original hatred, for she has learned how to say to the Lord with the words of David: "With perfect hatred have I hated them; they are reckoned enemies with me!"[28] He who hates his enemies with perfect hatred is he who sins neither in act nor in thought, which is a sign of the first and greatest dispassion.[29]

These "punches" thrown against the demons, which the irascible part of the soul dispenses, are thus praiseworthy and a sign of this irrational power's natural strength.[30] Evagrius therefore also recommends this method in prayer, which is the moment when the sins of anger take the most terrible vengeance.

> When you are tempted do not fall immediately to prayer. First utter some angry words against the one who afflicts you. The reason for this is found in the fact that your soul cannot pray purely when it is under the influence of various thoughts. By first speaking out in anger against them you confound and bring to nothing the devices of the enemy. To be sure this is the usual effect of anger even upon more worthy thoughts.[31]

Likewise, the "gnostic," who in himself should already be a master over the vices, still needs courage, as we have seen. Evagrius thus hits upon the following fine distinction:

> "A fool gives full vent to his anger, but a wise man quietly holds it back": Whoever "quietly holds back" a portion of his anger is either someone who gets angry [only] for a just cause, or someone who,

---

[28]Ps 138:22.
[29]M.c. 10.
[30]Cf. In Eccl. 7.3–7 (G.56).
[31]Pr. 42.

through patience, uses up part of his anger. Let one teach the former to the simple-minded and the latter to the zealous.[32]

The rule valid for all reads thus, that according to the words of the Prophet Joel (3:11, which Evagrius readily cites here), we should at once be "meek" and "a warrior": the former towards our fellow human beings, the latter towards the enemy, the "serpent."[33] Thus we will not harm our soul, as Evagrius learned from Macarius the Great.[34]

* *

The quotation from Joel teaches that we should not be satisfied with a mere attitude of resistance against the demons. In order to heal the diseased irascibility, a typically Christian love marked by meekness must come into play as a positive attitude. Since "love and hatred befall irascibility,"[35] it follows that "spiritual love"[36] "heals the burning part of irascibility."[37] Evagrius ceaselessly repeats this simple and yet so great a truth. "Wrath and hatred increase anger, but mercy and meekness lessen it even when [anger] is at hand."[38]

Man is "a spirit in a body,"[39] the latter of which is an integral component of the material cosmos "related" to him [and created with him].[40] The passions arise from the interrelation between the irrational powers tied to the body and the sensory world that surrounds us, when we find ourselves in the corresponding "receptivity" to them.

> The passions are accustomed to being stirred up by the senses, so that when charity [love] and continence are lodged in the soul, then the passions are not stirred up. And when they are absent the passions are stirred up. Anger stands more in need of remedies than

---

[32]*In Prov.* 29:11 (G.363).
[33]*Eul.* 10.
[34]*Pr.* 93.
[35]*KG* I.84.
[36]*Pr.* 35.
[37]*Gn.* 47.
[38]Cf. *Pr.* 20; cf. *KG* III.35.
[39]*Sk.* 35.
[40]*In Ps.* 43:20 ιβ.

concupiscence, and for that reason the love that is charity is to be reckoned a great thing indeed, in that it is able to bridle anger. The great and holy man Moses, where he treats of the things of nature, refers to it symbolically as the "killer of snakes."[41]

This "holy love"[42] (which is manifested in a variety of modes as compassion, mercy, goodness, humility, patience, beneficence, and above all as meekness) requires first of all on the part of whoever possesses it, or desires to acquire it, a fundamental readiness to forgive, as Christ himself taught us.

> Learn a lesson from the man who owed ten thousand talents: unless you forgive the man who owes you a debt, you yourself will not find forgiveness. For our Lord said: "He delivered him to the tormentors."[43]
>
> Explain this meekness [of Moses] to your brothers, and have [no] problem in accepting remorse over anger.[44]

Without this readiness to forgive—which in no way asks who is in the right—there is also no "pure prayer," for the resentment, the "remembrance of injuries" (μνησικακία), would undoubtedly defile the prayer, as we have seen.

> "Leave your gift before the altar and go be reconciled with your brother,"[45] our Lord said, and then you shall pray undisturbed. For resentment blinds the reason (ἡγεμονικόν) of the man who prays and casts a cloud over his prayer.[46]

Evagrius takes up the same Gospel text once more and develops the thought further.

---

[41]*Pr.* 38. Evagrius quotes 1 Cor 13:13 and Lev 11:22. The latter quotation is suggested by the name of the type of locust mentioned there, in Greek ὀφιομάχης, which literally means "fighter of snakes." "Snake" here refers of course to the demon that love is supposed to fight.

[42]*Ep.* 60.2, 4.

[43]*Or.* 104. Cf. Matt 18:24–35.

[44]*Ep.* 56:4 Gr.

[45]Matt 5:24.

[46]*Or.* 21.

If he who has need of nothing and who is not liable to be corrupted by any bribe does not receive the gift of a man who draws near to the altar before that man reconciles himself with his neighbor who has some grief against him,[47] then consider what great circumspection and [gift of] prudence we need if we are to offer incense that is well-pleasing to God on the spiritual altar.[48]

What is meant by "spiritual altar" is, of course, our intellect,[49] on which we offer our prayers to God like a fragrant offering of "incense."[50] And not just any prayers, but that highest and most perfect prayer "in spirit and in truth," which we, like the twenty-four elders of the Apocalypse, offer to the Lord in the "phial" of "perfect and spiritual love."[51] Consequently, what is at stake is the goal of the spiritual life itself!

*

Whoever reads the writings of Evagrius attentively will notice that he always—and without further reason—equates love with meekness. Yet what he understands by this virtue, unfortunately so unvalued today through constant misuse, is not difficult to see. Meekness has two sides, depending on how one looks at it.

"Remember, Lord, David and all his meekness": The Lord remembers the one in whom he enters,[52] and does not remember the one in whom he does not enter. When the Lord remembers meekness, then, one needs great angerlessness so that he might accept the Lord. Meekness then is steadfastness of irascibility, which comes about thanks to the renunciation of fleeting joys.[53]

---

[47]Cf. Matt 5:23 f.

[48]*Or.* 147.

[49]*In Ps.* 25:6 δ; cf. *KG* V.53; *Sk.* 6: "altar of incense."

[50]Cf. *Or.* 1; *O. Sp.* I.25. On prayer as the incense of the soul, cf. Clement of Alexandria, *Stromata* VII.32.5.

[51]*Or.* 77. Quotation: Rev 5:8.

[52]The following scholium shows what is meant by this expression: " 'Until I find a place for the Lord': the place of the Lord is the pure intellect" (*In Ps.* 131:5 β).

[53]*In Ps.* 131:1 α.

Meekness is in the first place an absence of anger and, consequently, a steadfastness (ἀταραξία) of irascibility against being aroused
in the midst of all temptations. But that is only one aspect. The David
named here is one of the Old Testament types of Christ, who said of
himself: "Learn from me for I am meek and lowly in heart."[54] The
other type, cited time and again, is Moses, about whom Scripture
reads, "Now the man Moses was very meek, above all the men who
were upon the face of the earth."[55] From Christ himself and from both
his Old Testament types, it is already clear that there is nothing at all
weak about this virtue of meekness. Rather, it is the virtue of the
strong. This is also how Evagrius sees his gnostic: as a man who is at
once "meek" and yet likewise energetic and "warlike," following the
words of the Prophet Joel (3:11): "Let the meek become a warrior."[56]

> Hold yourself in readiness to be meek and warlike: the former
> towards your kinsfolk, the latter towards the enemy. The [proper]
> use of irascibility consists of this: with enmity to do battle against
> the serpent.[57] And therein consists the mansuetude of the meek
> man: out of love to be forbearing with the brother, and to fight
> against [evil] thoughts. "Let the meek become a warrior," then,
> whereby his meekness is detached from deceitful thoughts, just as
> his militancy is from his relatives according to the flesh. Do not turn
> the use of anger against nature by being wroth with your brother
> "like a serpent,"[58] and instead being friends with the serpent by con-
> senting to the thoughts!
>
> The meek man does not refrain from love, even if he must suf-
> fer the worst. But for the sake of this [love] he is forbearing and
> patient, gentle and long-suffering.[59] For if forbearance is character-
> istic of love, it follows that angry quarreling is not. Anger awakens
> sorrow and hatred, but love attenuates all three.

---

[54]Matt 11:29.
[55]Num 12:3.
[56]*Ep.* 16.2; 24.2.
[57]Cf. Gen 3:15.
[58]Cf. Ps 57:4.
[59]Cf. 1 Cor 13:4–7.

If you stand firm in love, pay more heed to it than to the one who strikes you. Serve God with reverence and love: with the former insofar as he is Lord and Judge, and with the latter insofar as he loves mankind and nourishes them. He who has acquired the virtues of love imprisons the passions of the evil [demons], and whoever has received these three from the Holy Trinity—"faith, hope, and love"[60]—will be a city with a threefold wall, guarded by the virtues as by towers . . .[61]

*

From the example of Christ and both his Old Testament types, Moses and David, one can easily read wherein the nature of this "gentle strength" lies: neither in a weak yielding nor in the reckless playing out of one's own strength and superiority, but rather in submission of oneself, so that the other might have life. Scripture teaches us that "even a single holy man like Moses is able to avert the anger that bears down against an entire people!"[62]

Tell me, then, why has Scripture, when it wanted to praise Moses, left aside all miracles and commemorated only his meekness? For it does not say that Moses punished Egypt with the twelve plagues and led the esteemed people out thence. And Scripture does not say that Moses was the first to receive the Law, and that he acquired insights into bygone worlds.[63] And Scripture does not say that he separated the Red Sea with his staff, and brought forth water from the rock for the thirsting people. Rather, Scripture says that he stood all alone in the desert in the face of God, when he wanted to destroy Israel, and he besought to be blotted out with the sons of his people. Before God, he set down love for mankind and transgression by saying: "If thou wilt forgive their sin—and if not, blot me, I pray thee, out of thy book which thou hast written."[64] Thus spoke the meek one! But

---

[60] 1 Cor 13:13.
[61] *Eul.* 10.
[62] *In Ps.* 105:23 ια.
[63] Cf. footnote 71 below.
[64] Ex 32:32.

God preferred rather to forgive those who had sinned than to do an injustice to Moses.[65]

Thanks to this meekness, Moses was the only one who spoke with God "face to face"[66] and learned from him the reasons of creation[67] "in visible form, and not [only] in dark sayings."[68] For meek love, the "mother of knowledge,"[69] is the "door to natural knowledge,"[70] to which the five books of Moses bear witness.[71] Indeed, as "friendship with God" and "perfect spiritual love," love marked by meekness is even the place where "prayer in spirit and in truth is effected!"[72]

*

Love thus understood is a high ideal. In order to draw near to it progressively, small everyday steps are needed. In contrast with the demons, anger also manifests itself among men for the most part not in an ingrained attitude, but in small daily episodes. As always, Evagrius takes his lead here from Holy Scripture. "Wrath and anger turn love away, but gifts destroy resentment."[73]

The wise Solomon had already said this,[74] and Evagrius repeats it. As Solomon warns, the "gifts should be [given] in secret" when possible, lest "the left hand know what the right one is doing,"[75] thus ensuring that vainglory, which knows how to take advantage of every occasion, will not be able to worm its way in.

---

[65]*Ep.* 56.6.
[66]Ex 33:11.
[67]*Ep.* 27.3.
[68]Num 12:8.
[69]*Ep.* 27.2.
[70]*Pr.* Prologue (8).
[71]Moses as the composer of the book *On Nature*, i.e. creation (meant here is the book of Genesis); cf. *Pr.* 38; *KG* II.64; *Ep. Mel.*
[72]*Or.* 77.
[73]*Exhortation to a Virgin* (*Vg.*) 41.
[74]Prov 21:14.
[75]Matt 6:3; *In Prov.* 21:14 (G.225).

Gifts quench resentment; let Jacob persuade you of this. For he appeased Esau, who had come toward him with four hundred men,[76] through gifts . . .[77]

Meanwhile, only he who has at his disposal the necessary means can distribute gifts. "But as for ourselves [monks], who are poor men, we must make up for our lack of gifts by the table we lay,"[78] and this all the more so when we see our enemy "in the bitterest poverty."[79] Furthermore, the Bible verse to which Evagrius refers seems at first sight not to be exactly forgiving. "If your enemy is hungry, give him bread to eat; if thirsty, give him water to drink. For you will heap coals of fire on his head . . ."[80] Yet Evagrius is not at a loss in unlocking the "mystical meaning" of this passage, in that he explains it "intelligibly and spiritually"[81]: "by [thereby] purifying the intellect through kindness and doing good."[82] In the "intelligible and spiritual" understanding, the "fire" is not a means of destruction, but of purification and thus salvation for the sinner![83]

> If your brother irritates you,
> lead him into your house,
> and do not hesitate to go into his,
> but eat your morsel with him.
> For in doing this, you will deliver your soul
> and there will be no stumbling block for you at the hour of prayer.[84]

**

Whoever does not show this readiness to forgive is administered the bitter medicine of insult,[85] slander and contempt on the part of other

[76]Gen 32:6 ff.
[77]Cf. *Pr.* 26; cf. *Ant.* V.1.
[78]*Pr.* 26.
[79]Cf. *Ant.* V.28.
[80]Prov 25:21 f.
[81]*In Prov.* 23.1, 3 (G.250–51).
[82]*Ibid.* 25:21 f. (G.314).
[83]*In Ps.* 19:4 α et passim.
[84]*Mn.* 15.
[85]*Ep.* 51.2.

people by Christ, the wise "physician of souls," without having asked for it. These "remedies" cut into the flesh like a surgical branding iron,[86] cauterizing the infected wound and thus healing it. Here, meekness is put to its harshest test.

> [Speak] to the soul that does not understand that insults on the part of men result when God allows that it be tempted.[87]

To the soul tempted towards anger and revenge, Evagrius then quotes the example of the meek David, who humbly endured the curses of Shimei the Benjaminite![88] The true "gnostic" is also recognized by such demeanor.

> It is shameful for the gnostic to be involved in a lawsuit, whether as plaintiff or defendant: if as plaintiff, [it is shameful] because he will not have endured patiently; if as defendant, because he will have acted unjustly.[89]

We have already read something similar elsewhere.[90] Heavier still is the test when one is personally insulted and unjustly accused.[91] In this case, "we must pray for our enemies, lest we fall prey to resentment."[92] Likewise, we must stop the mouths of those who slander others in our presence.[93] Better yet, we ought to plug our own ears[94] and keep silent. As we shall yet see, Evagrius, from his own experience, knows very well whereof he speaks; he too was not spared unfair criticism and slander during his lifetime.[95] Instead of putting up a loudmouthed fight, he accepted the humiliation in silence—much to the astonishment of his contemporaries and even later generations—without resentment against his slanderers whom, by contrast, he

---

[86] *Ibid.* 52.2.
[87] *Ant.* V.8.
[88] 2 Sam 16:11 ff.
[89] *Gn.* 8.
[90] *M.c.* 32.
[91] *Gn.* 32.
[92] Cf. *In Ps.* 108:4 β.
[93] *Gn.* 32.
[94] *Eul.* 17.
[95] See under chapter 12.

regarded as his "benefactors." To him, quarrels were particularly and utterly odious.[96]

> Moreover, you wrote to me as if enemies were fighting with us. But I am not afraid of men; rather, I stand in fear of "Esau,"[97] lest he come by chance and beat me and "lay low the mother together with my children,"[98] slaying my intellect for its knowledge and rendering my mind childless, since it is robbed of the fruits of virtue. On the contrary, I call my visible enemies benefactors. Through their insults, they are the chastisers of my soul that craves for glory. I do not rebuke those who slander me, nor do I drive from me the physician of souls, who brings me health through the bandage of contempt. For I do know what happens to those who resist the physicians, how they tie them down with straps and operate on them against their will![99]

Abba Zosimas, who cites this text in the sixth century and comments on it, closes with the fitting words: "No one tells us the truth, except those who belittle us!"[100]

*

Through this bitter medicine, Christ—"the physician of the soul"—wants to lead man to renounce of his own free will all selfish desires. "Armed against anger, you will not submit to any desire. For such provides fuel for anger, and anger [then] clouds the noetic eye [of the soul] and ruins the state of prayer."[101]

Forming the object of these desires are all those occasions for anger we have already encountered: sustenance, clothing, possessions, and vainglory.[102] Whoever cuts off "these pretexts for irascibility" becomes unassailable by anger.[103] That is easy to see, for "as love

---

[96]*Ep.* 52.5, 7.
[97]Gen 32:11. Esau is a symbol of Satan; cf. *Ep. fid.* 1.13.
[98]I.e. the Logos of God in his role as physician (Matt 9:12); cf. *In Ps.* 106:20 θ.
[99]*Ep.* 52.4.
[100]Cf. G. Bunge, *Briefe aus der Wüste*, 79 f.
[101]Cf. *Or.* 27.
[102]*Ant.* V.30.
[103]Cf. *Pr.* 99.

rejoices in poverty, so hatred delights in riches."[104] "Indeed, the demon of anger flees when he does not succeed in disturbing [us] through wrath. On what account should one fall into wrath if he disdains food, riches, and vainglory?"[105]

*

As noble as the posited ideal may be, it never becomes extravagant and unrealistic. Even though "the work of love" consists "in showing itself to every image of God as being as nearly like its prototype as possible no matter how the demons ply their arts to defile them"[106] (for even the worst sinner remains "worthy of love as the image and his creation"[107]), Evagrius knows full well that "it is not possible to love all the brethren to the same degree" and that, lacking reciprocity of love, one must frequently be content with "associat[ing] with all in a manner that is above passion, that is to say, free of resentment and hatred."[108] This is also said about anger:

> "My heart grew hot within me": It is possible not to be angered when the demon of anger approaches us, but [it is] probably impossible not to burn.[109]

We must keep close watch over our heart[110] and may "not stand still" at the promptings of the demons,[111] for "it is not in our power to determine whether we are disturbed by these [tempting thoughts of the demons], but it is up to us to decide if they are to linger within us or not, and whether or not they are to stir up our passions."[112] This depends indeed on our own free "consent."[113]

---

[104] *Mn.* 16.
[105] *Ep.* 39.4.
[106] *Pr.* 89.
[107] *In Ps.* 118:113 v.
[108] *Pr.* 100.
[109] *In Ps.* 38:4 β.
[110] *Ep.* 11.3.
[111] *Ibid.* 55.2.
[112] *Pr.* 6.
[113] *Ibid.* 75.

Monastic wisdom that builds on experience also knows a very practical cure against these unintentional stirrings of anger:

> Patience and psalmody
> calm an assault of irascibility.[114]

Psalmody, a "charisma"[115] of no lesser significance than prayer,[116] forms a regular component in the life of the early monks. Their "Little Office" at the beginning and the end of night consisted in each case of twelve psalms, each one followed by a short prayer. During the day, the silent or half-loud "meditation" of a few psalm verses accompanied their manual labor and thereby prevented the mind from "straying" on account of not being occupied.[117] What is more, this psalmody—as experience teaches—also has a soothing effect on the passions in general[118] and on the provoked irascibility in particular. Evagrius mentions this characteristic quite often.

> Turbid anger is calmed by the singings of Psalms, by patience and almsgiving.[119]

> The songs inspired by the demons incite our desire and plunge our soul into shameful fancies. But "psalms and hymns and spiritual songs"[120] invite the spirit to the constant memory of virtue by cooling our boiling anger and by extinguishing our lusts.[121]

The "spiritual teaching"[122] contained in the Psalms urges the intellect to be virtuous, while all those parts of the Psalter (and there are a good number) that treat of "enemies" and "hostilities" of all sorts allow the intellect to direct its anger against the demons in accordance

---

[114]*Inst. mon.* (PG 79.1236A).
[115]*Or.* 87.
[116]Cf. *Pr.* 69.
[117]Cf. G. Bunge, *Earthen Vessels.*
[118]Cf. *Or.* 83.
[119]*Pr.* 15.
[120]Eph 5:19.
[121]*Pr.* 71; cf. *Mn.* 98; *M.c.* 27.24 ff.
[122]*In Ps.* 80:3 α.

with its nature.[123] Even the "Psalms of Imprecation," so unloved today and so frequently overlooked, have a healing power in the understanding of the early monks! This is naturally also known to the demons, and they cunningly turn our attention away from these texts and direct it to others.

> [Speak] to the demon who awakens anger against the brothers and then persuades us to sing that hymn in which is described the commandment of forbearance, which we have not kept. But he does this to ridicule us, because we psalmodize that commandment, which we have in fact not kept[124]: "How shall we sing the Lord's song in a foreign land?"[125]

One should carefully note such ruses of the demons if one does not want to fall into the same trap twice![126]

* *

As we have seen, one of the consequences of a provoked irascibility is recurrent nightmares and all sorts of similar terrors. They are a sure sign that the irascible part lacks not only the virtue of love but also that of courage.[127] What can be done to free oneself from these horrors? The knowledge of experience, which Evagrius owes to those monks "who have gone before us in the right manner," knows a very simple healing remedy: active love.

> [One of these fathers] delivered a certain brother from the disquieting spectres by which he was visited in the night by ordering him to minister to the sick and to fast while he did it. When asked about his rationale for employing this procedure, he replied: "Such afflictions are extinguished by no other remedy so well as by mercy."[128]

---

[123] *Pr.* 93 et passim.
[124] *Ant.* V.13. An almost identical text is found in *In Ps.* 136:3 β.
[125] Ps 136:4.
[126] *M.c.* 9.26 ff.
[127] Cf. *Pr.* 89.
[128] *Ibid.* 91.

The same patristic wisdom has also entered other writings, albeit without any indication of the source. An example of this can be seen in the *Antirrhetikos*, where the monk—in the words of Psalm 118:98 ff.—thanks the Lord for having come to understand that these frightening nightly visions "are extinguished through mercy and forbearance."[129] Aside from "uninterrupted prayer,"[130] Evagrius therefore frequently mentions this active brotherly love.

> "If you sit down, you will not be afraid; when you lie down, your sleep will be sweet. And you will not be afraid of alarm coming upon you, nor of approaching attacks of the ungodly": By this we know that compassion dispels the terrifying visions that befall us at night. Meekness, angerlessness, patience, and everything that is able to pacify the aroused irascibility, have the same effect, since these visions of terror tend to arise from the provocation of irascibility.[131]

---

[129]*Ant.* V.12.
[130]*M.c.* 23.33.
[131]*In Prov.* 3:24–25 (G.36).

CHAPTER 9

"Pure Prayer"

A s Evagrius has taught us to understand, anger is an ominous, "demonic" passion—and not merely metaphorically speaking. It destroys not only interpersonal relationships, but also our relationship to God. It confuses not only our psyche (a fact which last but not least finds expression in fearful nightmares), but at the "time for prayer" it also "blinds" our intellect, the place where we directly encounter God. For the intellect is by its very nature made to pray, even without this material body.[1] Prayer prepares the intellect to practice the activity proper to it,[2] i.e. the "contemplation of divine knowledge."[3] Thus, "prayer is activity which is appropriate to the dignity of the spirit; or better, it is appropriate for its nobler and adequate operation"[4]: in other words, "its highest intellectual act."[5] Yet anger annihilates all this; one can thus rightly say that it destroys man's true goal. With good reason, Evagrius warns:

> If you restrain your anger, you yourself will be spared and in the process prove yourself . . . wise . . . [and] will be counted among the men of prayer.[6]

Here is not the place to expound in detail the Evagrian teaching on "true prayer."[7] In this context, we will deal with a single yet truly

---

[1] *Pr.* 49.
[2] *Or.* 83.
[3] *Ibid.* 86.
[4] *Ibid.* 84.
[5] *Ibid.* 34.
[6] *Ibid.* 26.
[7] Cf. G. Bunge, *Das Geistgebet: Studien zum Traktat* De Oratione *des Evagrios*

essential aspect that has already been repeatedly mentioned: the purity of prayer. Of all passions, anger defiles this purity most enduringly.

*

In Evagrius' works, "purity" is always a synonym for "impassibility" (ἀπάθεια).

> "He will reward me according to the purity of my hands": "Purity of hands" means the impassibility of the soul, which is achieved through God's grace and man's zeal.[8]

Like everything in life, ἀπάθεια—the freedom not from the assaults of the demons, but rather from the tyranny of the passions— also develops gradually. Accordingly, Evagrius distinguishes between a "holy,"[9] or "first and greatest"[10] passionlessness, and an "imperfect" or "little" one.[11]

> Perfect purity of heart develops in the soul after the victory over all the demons, whose function it is to offer opposition to the ascetic life. But there is designated an imperfect purity of heart in consideration of the power of the demon that meantime fights against it,[12]

or also inasmuch as this first stage cleanses only the "desiring part of the soul"[13] and thus only one of the two irrational powers. Whoever wants to pray "as one ought"[14] must therefore pray "to be purified from the passions."[15]

But in order to be able really to pray "purely and without being led astray,"[16] one must not only "free [one]self of every thought that is

---

Pontikos. Schriftenreihe des Zentrums Patristischer Spiritualität—Koinonia im Erzbistum Köln 25 (Cologne: Luthe-Verlag, 1987).

[8]*In Ps.* 17:21 ιβ; cf. *KG* I.79.
[9]*M.c.* 3.37.
[10]*Ibid.* 10.15.
[11]Cf. *ibid.* 15.1.
[12]*Pr.* 60.
[13]*M.c.* 16.5.
[14]Rom 8:26; cf. *Or.* 20, 24, 49, 51.
[15]*Or.* 37.
[16]*Ibid.* 73.

colored by passion,"[17] but eventually of any mental image whatsoever, "for prayer is the rejection of [all] concepts,"[18] as Evagrius quite finely evinces.[19] "Perfect impassibility" or "purity" is thus deliverance not only from passionate deeds and thoughts, but also a "transcending of all thoughts of [created] things,"[20] for praying is "a continual inter-course of the spirit with God . . . without intermediary."[21] Nothing so threatens this purity, even at its lowest level, as does anger. "If you long for pure prayer, be on guard against anger!"[22]

For as soon as the one who prays has begun to pray "without being distracted" by any mental images, "then there commences an all-out battle day and night against the irascible part [of the soul]."[23] The demons now spare no effort to divert the intellect from the "thought of God." In this assault, one of their most powerful allies is our mem-ory (μνήμη), in which the mental images of the things of this cre-ation, with which our intellect is naturally occupied, are "imprinted" like a seal in soft wax.

> When you pray, keep your memory under close custody. Do not let it suggest your own fancies to you, but rather have it convey the awareness of your reaching out to God. Remember this: the mem-ory has a powerful proclivity for causing detriment to the spirit at the time of prayer.[24]

These "thieves" who "rob" us here[25] are the demons, naturally; they are able to exert a direct influence on our memory,[26] and prefer to do this especially through thoughts of anger.

---

[17] *Ibid.* 4.
[18] *Ibid.* 70.
[19] *Ibid.* 56–58.
[20] *Sk.* 23.
[21] *Or.* 3.
[22] *M.c.* 43.1.
[23] *Pr.* 63.
[24] *Or.* 44.
[25] Cf. Let Jer 17.
[26] *Or.* 10, 47.

> When you are at prayer, the memory activates fantasies (φαντασίας)
> of either past happenings or of fresh concerns, or else the face of
> someone whom you have distressed.[27]

This "face of someone whom [we] have distressed" is that "image"
(εἰκών) of a sensual man that ascends unintentionally in our mind at
the time of prayer and with which the intellect then (on account of
this image reviving a hidden passion) "says or does something secretly
in lawless manner"[28] instead of holding intimate "converse" with
God. This is not only a caricature of "true prayer," but also pure idolatry, since the one who prays deifies (θεοποιῶν), as it were, "the face
of the enemy." "For what the mind constantly looks upon during
prayer should rightly be acknowledged as its god."[29] The one whom
such a thing befalls is truly "far removed from pure prayer"![30] An
attempt should be made to prevent this in good time.

> So let us avoid this disease of malicious talk, beloved, let us have no
> evil memory against anyone, nor make faces at the memory of a
> brother. For evil demons eagerly watch our every movement and
> leave nothing unexplored that could be used against us, whether our
> sitting, or our getting up, our standing, our walk, our words or our
> look. They are always curious, devising "deceits all the day"[31] in order
> to put to shame the humble mind and to extinguish its blessed light
> during prayer.[32]

Consequently, one approaches "pure prayer" in the same manner
as impassibility—gradually. First of all, such prayer must be free of all
passionate thoughts[33] as well as all "mental images" of created
things.[34] But even that is not enough! This prayer must also grow free
of the "contemplation" (θεωρία) of the reasons (λόγοι) of these

---

[27] *Ibid.* 45.
[28] *Sk.* 13
[29] *M.c.* 37.24 f.
[30] *Ibid.* 5.17 f.; 16.31 f.
[31] Ps 37:13.
[32] *M.c.* 37.26–35.
[33] *Or.* 54.
[34] *Ibid.* 56.

things,[35] since they make the intellect itself "multiplex" on account of their own multiplicity.[36] In short, whoever wants to hold "continual intercourse of the spirit with God . . . without intermediary" (i.e. directly from person to person) must proceed "free from all matter [and] draw near the immaterial Being."[37]

> "Let my prayer arise in thy sight as incense": Like incense does the prayer arise of him who can say: "For we are the aroma of Christ to God among those who are being saved and among those who are perishing."[38] And there is one form of prayer, which leaves the intellect without impress: the converse of the intellect with God. I call an intellect un-impressed which, at the time of prayer, does not imagine anything bodily (μηδὲν σωματικὸν . . . φανταζόμενον). For only those names and words that signify something sensual imprint and mold our intellect. In prayer, the intellect must be free of everything sensual. But the thought of God leaves the mind of necessity without imprint, since [God] is not a body.[39]

Our prayer is, as it were, a well-pleasing sacrifice of incense,[40] which we offer to God on the "spiritual altar"[41] of our intellect.[42] But in order for this sacrifice[43] to be well-pleasing to God, both the "altar" and the "gift" must be completely "pure." Evagrius thus calls blessed the intellect "that attains to perfect formlessness (ἀμορφία) at the time of prayer"[44] and "complete unconsciousness of all sensible experience."[45] Why? Because this condition alone makes the intellect "deaf" and "dumb"[46] to all demonic whispers,[47] which—as we have

---

[35] *Ibid.* 57.
[36] *Ibid.*
[37] *Ibid.* 66.
[38] 2 Cor 2:15.
[39] *In Ps.* 140:2 α.
[40] *Or.* 1; cf. *ibid.* 76, 77, 141.
[41] *Ibid.* 147.
[42] *In Ps.* 25:6 δ; *Sk.* 6 et passim.
[43] Cf. *Pr.* 23.
[44] *Or.* 117.
[45] *Ibid.* 120.
[46] Ps 37:14.
[47] *Or.* 11.

seen—always take their starting point from something sensual. Yet nothing defiles the "purity" once acquired in the eyes of God more than anger.

> The prayer of the angry man
> is an "abominable thing of incense,"[48]
> and the psalmody of the enraged man
> [is] a hateful dissonance.[49]
>
> The gift of the resentful man
> is a sacrifice "spoiled by ants,"[50]
> and does not draw near
> the blessed "altar."[51]

Whoever longs for "pure prayer" must avoid not only sins of anger in thought and deed; he must also purify his memory—not only in general from all that is sensual, but especially from every recollection of injustices suffered. Whether and to what extent he has been successful in this may be ascertained by what he beholds in dreams, since sleep with its dreams is the mirror of our conscious life, so to speak.

> We shall now inquire how, in the fantasies that occur during sleep, the demons imprint shapes and forms on our intellect. Normally, the intellect receives these shapes and forms either through the eyes when it is seeing, or through the ears when it is hearing, or through some other sense, or else through the memory, which stirs up and imprints on the intellect things it has experienced through the body.
>
> Now it seems to me that in our sleep, when the activity of our bodily senses is suspended, it is by arousing the memory that the demons make this imprint. But, in that case, how do the demons arouse the memory? Is it through the passions? Clearly this is so, for those in a state of purity and dispassion no longer experience demonic fantasies in sleep.

---

[48]Is 1:13.
[49]*O. Sp.* 4.18.
[50]Lev 22:22.
[51]*O. Sp.* 4.19.

There is also an activity of the memory that is not demonic: it is caused by ourselves or by the angelic powers, and through it we may meet with saints and delight in their company. We should notice in addition that during sleep, the memory stirs up without the body's participation those very images (εἴδωλα) that the soul has received in association with the body. This is clear from the fact that we often experience such images during sleep, when the body is at rest.[52]

In sleep, then, there arise in us out of the memory all that we have absorbed at one time or another. But this is not all that happens: the door to another world also opens to us. According to our inner condition, we then encounter the demons who frighten us with fearful images of the imagination, and this happens especially to the angry.[53] Otherwise, we encounter the saints and have "dream visions of angels" marked by a "great calmness of soul and ineffable joy . . . but during the day by the absence of passionate thoughts and [the presence of] pure prayer."[54]

As we have seen, this happens to the pure and the passionless.

> A patient man
> beholds visions, gatherings of holy angels,
> and whoever harbors no resentment
> trains in spiritual reasons,
> and at night he receives
> the key to mysteries.[55]

Nonetheless, it would certainly be a mistake to think that demonic dream visions or, generally speaking, nightly terrors plague angry people exclusively. It is precisely the "spiritual teacher" whom the demons plague most vehemently at night.[56] His blessed impassibility is put to the harshest test here and proves itself through perfect imperturbability at this insurrection of hell.[57] The true "gnostic" pos-

[52]*M.c.* 4.1–18.
[53]*Ibid.* 27.20.
[54]*Ibid.* 28.27 ff.
[55]*O. Sp.* 4.21.
[56]*Or.* 139.
[57]*M.c.* 29.

sesses in full measure not only the virtue of "spiritual love," but also that of courage and endurance, which enable him "to know no fear of enemies and eagerly to endure afflictions."[58] Consequently, such terrors befall the perfect not only at night, but during prayer as well. In his treatise *On Prayer*, Evagrius hands down several such occurrences that may appear to many as being utterly unbelievable.[59] One may suffice here. It recalls to us those nightmares of the angry, of which we have spoken in detail. But how differently the nameless saint reacts to these terrors here!

> We once heard a story about one of the holy men of prayer who was assailed by the spiteful demon. No sooner had he lifted his hands in prayer than this demon transformed himself into a lion and, raising his forelegs up, he sunk his claws into either cheek of this athlete of prayer. But this man simply would not yield. He did not lower them until he had completed all his usual prayers.[60]

---

[58] *Pr.* 89.
[59] *Or.* 106–112.
[60] *Ibid.* 106.

CHAPTER 10

Dialogue with God

Anger and "pure prayer" are direct opposites and mutually exclusive—so much is clear. The former is, as it were, a caricature of the latter. For while at prayer—if one may even call it that—the angry man constantly has before his spiritual eyes the "image" of him who offended him or to whom he himself has caused grief, thereby making him into a "god" (or idol),[1] the true man of prayer "loses himself" entirely "in being together with God," in converse with him alone.[2] Only when one has fully grasped what this means can one realize what anger robs a person of.

*

> Prayer is a continual intercourse of the spirit with God. What state of soul, then, is required, that the spirit might thus strain after its Master without wavering, living constantly with him without intermediary?[3]

In his treatise *On Prayer*,[4] Evagrius adopts a felicitous definition of prayer from Clement of Alexandria[5] and develops it further. Here we touch upon the centerpiece of the Evagrian teaching on "true prayer," which undoubtedly is also based on personal experience. Like Clement,[6] Evagrius in this definition also has in mind Moses, as will

---

[1] *M.c.* 37.24 f.
[2] *Or.* 34.
[3] *Ibid.* 3.
[4] The same definition also appears in *In Ps.* 140:1 α and *Sk.* 28; thus, it is important for Evagrius.
[5] *Stromata* VII.39.6.
[6] Cf. *ibid.* VI.104.1.

become still clearer.[7] The intellect is granted that state (κατάστασις), which it here requires, through "the quartet of virtues."[8] These four virtues, when present in their "fullness," "unify the soul."[9] This is particularly accomplished, however, through meekness, that most excellent virtue of Moses,[10] for "prayer is a scion of meekness and angerlessness."[11] But meekness (or love) is itself "a scion of impassibility," which in turn is the "blossom of the practical life," the foundation of which life is "the keeping of the commandments."[12] The following chapter leads us one step further into the mystery of prayer.

> If Moses, when he attempted to draw near the burning bush, was prohibited until he should remove the shoes from his feet,[13] how should you not free yourself of every thought that is colored by passions, seeing that you wish to see One who is beyond every thought and perception?[14]

"Prayer," then, is both these things: "seeing" God and "holding converse" with him— becoming his "collocutor" (συνόμιλος). For both, Moses is the Old Testament type pointing forward to the future reality, for he was indeed allowed to see God, although only from behind.[15] Nevertheless, he was permitted to speak with him "face to face, as a man speaks to his friend."[16] "Seeing" therefore effects a greater nearness and directness than does "speaking."

The full reality of what was granted to Moses as a type was revealed only in the New Covenant. For Moses did not yet know what—or rather, who—this "face of God" was, how "seeing" was to be understood, and how "speaking" with God was possible "without

---

[7]See *Or.* 4.
[8]*Ibid.* 1.
[9]*Ibid.* 2.
[10]Num 12:3.
[11]Cf. *Or.* 14.
[12]*Pr.* 81.
[13]Ex 3:2–5.
[14]*Or.* 4.
[15]Ex 33:18 ff.
[16]*Ibid.* 33:11.

intermediary." The Son who became man was the first to grant to us access to the Father, since he is the perfect "image of God"[17] and the only true "exegete"[18] of the Father.[19] Indeed, who could turn to the Father "without intermediary" if not the Son! Man is only made capable of doing this when he has accepted faith in the Only-Begotten Son[20] and has himself become an adopted son of the Father by virtue of his incorporation into the Son's mystical body through holy baptism. This adoption is the work of the Holy Spirit, that "other Comforter" whom the Son has besought for us from the Father. Thus, he it is also who enables and authorizes the one who prays to raise the voice of the Son and like him to cry, "Abba, Father,"[21] as we do in that prayer which the Only-Begotten One himself taught us.

> If you wish to pray, then it is God's [help that] you need. He it is "who gives prayer to the man who prays."[22] On that account call upon him saying: "Hallowed be thy name, thy kingdom come,"[23] that is, the Holy Spirit and thine Only-Begotten Son. This is what our Lord taught us when he said[24]: "The Father is adored in spirit and in truth."[25]

*

"No one has ever seen God."[26] However, thanks to the Son's Incarnation, the Christian may "in true prayer" behold this "face of the Father in heaven," the sight of whom is reserved for the angels alone.[27]

---

[17] 2 Cor 4:4; Col 1:15. Cf. *In Ps.* 16:2 α; 79:8 δ.
[18] John 1:18.
[19] *Ibid.* 14:6.
[20] *Ibid.* 1:12 et passim.
[21] Rom 8:15.
[22] 1 Kgs 2:8.
[23] Matt 6:9.
[24] John 4:23.
[25] Cf. *Or.* 59.
[26] John 1:18.
[27] Matt 18:10, cf. *In Ps.* 29:8 ζ.

By true prayer, a monk becomes another angel,[28] for he ardently longs to see the face of the Father in heaven.[29]

"To see the face of the Father in heaven" means to behold the Son[30] and in him the Father. For it is written: "He who has seen me has seen the Father."[31] This "seeing" is not a sensory, visionary process, for "to behold" means "to recognize,"[32] since both concepts are synonymous.[33] Whoever longs, then, to behold the Father's face puts all his effort towards this end—to beholding the Son[34]—and there is nothing the demons try to thwart so much as this "seeking" of the Son![35]

*

Only he who sees his opposite has drawn near to him.[36] From this nearness, this "being together" (συνουσία),[37] there arises then that "converse with God" the Father, whose Old Testament type was Moses, but whose fullness was first revealed to us by the Son.

The man who loves God[38] constantly lives and speaks with him as a Father. He turns aside from every thought that is tinged with passion.[39]

This "direct discourse" with the Father is only possible in his Holy Spirit and his Only-Begotten Son,[40] as we have seen. Whoever has learned, by God's grace, "to pray as one ought"[41] has indeed become a "theologian,"[42] since he "no longer honors the Creator because of

---

[28]Luke 20:36.
[29]Or. 113.
[30]In Ps. 16:2 α.
[31]John 14:9.
[32]In Ps. 23:6 γ.
[33]Ibid. 68:29 ιζ.
[34]Or. 51.
[35]Ibid. 50.
[36]Ep. Mel. 3 f.
[37]Or. 34.
[38]Deut 6:6.
[39]Or. 54.
[40]Ibid. 58.
[41]Rom 8:26; cf. Or. 20, 24, 49, 51.
[42]Or. 60.

his works, but praises him because of himself."[43] For the Son and the Spirit, the only true and eternal "mediators" between the Father and his creation,[44] are themselves not creatures. Rather, they are "true God of true God," as is said in the Nicene Creed (381 AD). Accordingly, this is man's destiny already on earth! But nothing robs him so greatly of his true vocation as does anger. Thus, whoever allows himself to be dominated by the demon of anger not only becomes a "demon" himself, but also must simply have lost his mind.

> No one who loves true prayer and yet gives way to anger or resentment can be absolved from the imputation of madness. For he resembles a man who wishes to see clearly and for this purpose he scratches his eyes.[45]

Elsewhere, he speaks more drastically of this "darkening" of sight:

> Whoever . . . is easily moved to anger is like a man who pierces himself in the eyes with a metal stylus.[46]

This is more than merely a metaphor. As we have seen, the soul possesses two "eyes," like the body. With the left eye, the soul contemplates God's creatures; with the right, "she beholds the blessed light of the Holy Trinity at the time of prayer."[47] If both "eyes" are blinded, the "light of the eyes"[48]—that is, the light of the intellect itself[49]—is also extinguished, as is that "blessed light of the Holy Trinity," which it beheld. Yet this is the death of prayer, since:

> Prayer is an intellectual state that arises only through the light of the Holy Trinity.[50]

[43]*Ibid.* 59.
[44]*Ep. Mel.* 31.
[45]*Or.* 64.
[46]*Gn.* 5; cf. *M.c.* 32.15 f.
[47]*M.c.* 42.6 f.
[48]Ps 37:10.
[49]*Inst. mon. suppl.* 10.
[50]*Sk.* 27.

"Light" in Evagrius' works is first of all undoubtedly a biblical symbol of knowledge. Already in Hosea 10:12, we read, "Kindle for yourselves a light of knowledge." But when Evagrius speaks of the "appearance of that light . . . which makes 'the place of God' known,"[51] and when he designates the "illuminated intellect" itself as God's "dwelling place,"[52] then it becomes clear that he is speaking here of a direct, personal experience of God—"in a mirror, as it were"[53]—of one's own self that is created "in the image of God." Evagrius always speaks only in biblical-symbolic phrases of this mystical experience in the highest sense, which undoubtedly was also granted to him.

> The state of the intellect is an intelligible height, resembling the color of heaven, which is also granted the light of the Holy Trinity at the time of prayer.[54]

In the background of this and related texts (the symbolic meaning of which cannot be more closely deciphered here) stands the sublime experience of God at Sinai, of which Exodus 24:9 ff. speaks. There, the elders of Israel together with Moses saw "the place where the God of Israel stood, beneath whose feet there was what looked like a sapphire pavement pure as the firmament itself in its purity." The intellect, cleansed of all passions, has exactly this experience: that is, "it beholds itself resembling the color of sapphire or of heaven" when God "breathes into it the related light."[55]

> When the intellect "has put off the old man and put on [the new man], born of grace,"[56] then at the time of prayer it will behold its own condition as resembling the color of sapphire or of heaven. In Scripture, this same [condition] is called "the place of God," which the elders beheld on Mount Sinai.[57]

---

[51] *M.c.* 40.7 ff.
[52] *Sk.* 25.
[53] *Inst. mon. suppl.* 13.
[54] *Sk.* 4.
[55] *Ibid.* 2.
[56] Eph 4:24; Col 3:9 f. The heart of the matter here is baptism!
[57] *M.c.* 39.

However, this "heavenly state" of the intellect is destroyed by thoughts arising from anger: suspicion, hatred, and resentment, which "blind" the intellect more than all others.[58] They "extinguish" this "blessed light" of the intellect.[59]

> In pure thoughts, [there] is imprinted a splendid sky to see and a spacious region where to a certain extent[60] the reasons (λόγοι) of beings are beheld and the holy angels approach those who are worthy. And this vision that is imprinted—resentment causes it to be seen [only] obscurely, and anger when it flames up destroys it completely.[61]

Anger blots out not only the knowledge of the "reasons of beings" but also the "blessed light of the Holy Trinity" and the knowledge thereof. Indeed, whoever through his own fault has deprived himself of this sublime experience of God and his creation must have lost his mind.

---

[58] *Ibid.* 32.3 ff.

[59] *Ibid.* 37.35.

[60] The text of *KG* V.39 uses the expression *v'aikana* here, which A. Guillaumont translates as "how" (*comment*). In contrast, *Ep.* 39.5 (containing a slightly different version of the same text) reads *k'ma hu*, which W. Frankenberg quite fittingly translates as ποσῶς. Such reductions are also found elsewhere in Evagrius' works; cf. e.g. *Pr.* 53 and 55.

[61] *KG* V.39.

CHAPTER II

The Virtue of the Angels

The image of man, as presented by Evagrius, would remain one-sided were one only to present it against the dark background of those vices that pervert it, without also showing its luminous, "angelic" dimensions. Furthermore, hardly anyone could muster the courage and endurance to do battle against a vice such as anger if he did not have an appealing image of real humanness before his eyes—an ideal which perhaps he is not able to develop, but which nevertheless widens the narrow horizon of our earthly existence. A good deal has already been mentioned in the preceding chapters, but here we shall attempt to form a synthesis.

*

> Patience: the armor of understanding,
> judgment over wrath,
> sanatorium of the heart,
> exhortation of the insolent,
> pacification of the agitated,
> storm-free haven,
> comfort of the grieved,
> kindness toward all.
> When slandered, it blesses;
> mistreated, it rejoices.
> Consolation of the oppressed,
> mirror of hoped-for good things,
> trophy of the tortured.[1]

---

[1] *Vita* (PG 79.1144A–B).

The vices are nothing other than the perverted functioning of the soul's three powers, and this point cannot be repeated often enough. In order to fight effectively against a vice, one must thus practice the opposing virtue. In the case of anger, this is forbearance—one of the manifestations of meek love, as Evagrius outlines above. We have already seen that this meek love is in no way weak. Among all the virtues, it is the one that grants mankind access to God and his mysteries.

> "Make me to know thy ways, O Lord; teach me thy paths": Whoever desires to know the "ways of the Lord" must become meek: for it says, "He will teach the meek his ways."[2] But the meek are those who have brought to an end the endless struggle of irascibility and desire in the soul, as well as the struggle of the passions caused by these.[3]

That meekness is an "aristocratic virtue," in the best sense of the term, has already been made clear—according to the witness of Scripture, it is a distinguishing mark of the ruling figures of Moses,[4] David,[5] and Christ.[6] This being the case, Evagrius makes use especially of Moses to sketch the figure of his true "gnostic," to whom knowledge of God and his creation was granted on account of his meekness. David, on the other hand, is the type of one who is "like the angels." In both cases, Evagrius naturally proceeds from Scripture as he understands it—that is, "intelligibly and spiritually."[7] In the preceding pages, Moses was more often the topic of discussion. Here, we shall turn to this man who is "like the angels": David.

*

> "When shall I come and behold the face of God?": If the "angels always behold the face of the Father,"[8] but this one [who prays]

---

[2] Ps 24:9.
[3] *In Ps.* 24:4 γ.
[4] Num 12:3.
[5] Ps 131:1.
[6] Matt 11:29.
[7] *In Prov.* 23:1, 3 (G.251).
[8] Matt 18:10.

desires to behold the face of God, then David consequently desires to become an angel.[9]

Does David thereby desire the impossible? Not in the least, as Evagrius again culls from Scripture.

"The light of thy countenance has shone upon us, Lord": The angels always behold the face of God, but mankind beholds the light of his countenance. The face of the Lord is the spiritual contemplation of everything that has come into being on this earth, while the light of his countenance is a partial knowledge even of these things, if [it is true that] according to [the word[10]] of the wise woman from Tekoa, David was like an angel of the Lord, perceiving all things on earth.[11]

David naturally became such an "angel of God" through his great meekness,[12] "for this is the virtue of the angels!"[13]

Kindness and meekness are the cherubim of the soul.[14]

Consequently, ever since the time of the Old Covenant, it has been an established fact that certain people, thanks to their great "purity of heart,"[15] have the ability to attain an "almost angelic state"[16] and, what is more, to become "equal to the angels (ἰσάγγελος)"[17] through "true prayer." This then advances them to the level of eating the desired[18] "bread of the angels," that is, to participate in the God-knowledge of the angels.

"Man ate the bread of angels": The Redeemer says: "I am the bread which came down from heaven."[19] The angels ate this bread first,

---

[9] *In Ps.* 41:3 α.
[10] 2 Kgs 14:20, 36.
[11] *In Ps.* 4:7 ζ.
[12] Cf. Ps 131:1.
[13] *Vita* K.
[14] *Sent.* 42.
[15] *In Ps.* 141:8 ε.
[16] *Ibid.* 118:171 οθ.
[17] *Or.* 113.
[18] *In Ps.* 23:6 γ.
[19] John 6:51.

but now mankind as well. "Eating" here means "to recognize," for the intellect "eats" what it recognizes, and does not "eat" what it does not recognize.[20]

After all that we have heard up to now, it is clear that this "almost angelic condition" consists in "imitating the angelic mode."[21] For if man is in himself "like a child that stands between justice and injustice," neither an angel nor a demon, "until the consummation of the age,"[22] he is of course free to share the life of the angels or that of the demons.[23] If he drinks the forbidden "dragon's wine" (anger with all its consequences), he becomes a "demon," a "serpent,"[24] already in this present time. Yet if he acquires the angelic virtue of meek love, he becomes "like an angel." Let us now examine more closely wherein this "angelic resemblance" consists and to whom it is granted.

*

In the Old Covenant, "some people recognized the reasons of the things on earth"[25]—for example, Moses and David, as we have already seen. By contrast, in the New Testament this knowledge is in principle open to all who are baptized, especially those "who have believed in Christ"[26] and received "the spiritual seal"[27]—that is, that "anointing" of the Holy Spirit, who reveals God's mysteries to them.[28] These are the "sons of the Resurrection," who Christ said would not die and would become "like angels."[29]

This "angelic resemblance" is an eschatological good, and Evagrius is naturally also aware of this. However, like all eschatological goods of salvation, this one is already experienced here on earth by

---

[20]*In Ps.* 77:25 ι.
[21]*Or.* 39.
[22]*In Prov.* 1:32 (G.16); cf. *KG* IV.13.
[23]*KG* III.76.
[24]*Ep.* 56.4, 5.
[25]*KG* I.23.
[26]*Ibid.* V.6; cf. Gal 2:16 and Heb 12:22.
[27]*Mn.* 124.
[28]*In Ps.* 118:131 ν θ.
[29]Luke 20:36.

God's grace—a "guarantee," so to speak, of the glory to come.[30] As we have already seen, this experience is made in "true prayer"[31] and especially that "true worship of the Father in spirit and in truth,"[32] which Christ describes as now abolishing the cult of the Old Covenant and every way of worshipping God on account of His coming.[33] This is so, since an angel stands in close relationship not only to the "beholding of the face of the Father in heaven," but also to the prayer "in spirit and in truth."

> The statement in the Apocalypse that speaks of the angel who takes care of putting incense in the bowl that contains the prayer of the saints[34] refers, in my opinion, to precisely this grace wrought by the angel. He infuses knowledge of true prayer so that for the future the spirit may stand firm, free of all acedia and all negligence.[35]

"That grace" refers back to the preceding chapter (*Or.* 74) where it is said that "when the angel of the Lord visits us, he dispels by his word alone every conflicting force [of the demon] acting in us, and brings it about that the light of our spirit operates without deception." In other words, the "light" of his ability to recognize things is now no longer darkened, but can freely develop. Here we learn that this recognition aims at "true prayer" and the "worship of the Father in spirit and truth," that is, in his Holy Spirit and his Only-Begotten Son.[36]

The angel of the Lord is able to mediate such sublime knowledge to us since he not only "knows all things on earth"[37] and predicts the future (as in the book of Daniel), but also "always beholds the face of the Father in heaven."[38] But through his "true prayer," man, in his desire to behold this same face, becomes himself "like an angel."[39]

---

[30]2 Cor 1:22 ff.
[31]*Or.* 113.
[32]*Ibid.* 58.
[33]John 4:23.
[34]Rev 8:3.
[35]*Or.* 75.
[36]*Ibid.* 59.
[37]*In Ps.* 4:7 ζ.
[38]Cf. *Or.* 80.
[39]*Ibid.* 113.

The next chapter will conclude this thought and will also name the conditions for this exaltation of man.

> The phials of perfume are said to be the prayers of the saints, which are offered by the twenty-four elders.[40] These phials are to be understood as the love of God, or rather as the perfect and spiritual charity in which prayer is offered in spirit and truth.[41]

* *

These "saints," to whom this "friendship with God" (which at the same time is also friendship with the holy powers, i.e. the angels[42]) was granted, are above all those of whom Holy Scripture speaks as "friends of God." In the Old Covenant, these are Abraham[43] and Moses[44]; in the New Covenant, John the Baptist[45] and the Apostles.[46] Thereafter, these friends are all those who were made worthy of the "grace of the knowledge of true prayer." For Evagrius, these are first of all those whom he calls "spiritual fathers" and who "are to be honored like the angels."[47] From their lives, we see excellent examples of what Evagrius understands by an "angelic man," since they have been granted that knowledge that characterizes the angels.[48] With regard to their spiritual children, these fathers play a role analogous to that entrusted to the angels in general towards mankind.

> Know that God watches over everything through Christ, and that [Christ], in turn, carries out his providence over everything through the holy angels who possess in exceeding abundance knowledge "of the things on earth" . . .[49]

---

[40]Rev 5:8.
[41]*Or.* 76–77.
[42]*In Prov.* 10:18 (G.120).
[43]Jas 2:23; cf. *In Prov.* 19:4 (G.189).
[44]Ex 33:11.
[45]John 3:29.
[46]John 15:15; cf. *In Prov.* 6:1 (G.69).
[47]*Pr.* 100.
[48]Cf. *KG* V.7.
[49]*In Eccl.* 5.7–11 (G.38).

Consequently, God accomplishes the work of his providence over the world in manifold ways through the "hand" of the angels.[50] The "worlds" of angels and demons are, of course, not directly accessible to us[51]; we can see neither angels nor demons[52] as they really are, and in the case of angels, we also should not even wish to see them,[53] since such "apparitions" are all too often only a demonic deceit.[54] Whoever falls for this runs the risk of losing his mind. In order to become visible to us, the demons gladly assume alien bodies,[55] transforming thereafter into "angels of light" in order to deceive us.[56]

In an invisible way, mankind is entrusted to the guidance of the holy angels.[57] Additionally, every person has his own personal guardian angel "who is assigned to him from youth on."[58] They are our guides to whom we are entrusted from the beginning. [59]

The task of the angels—who naturally see us quite well[60] and can also draw near to our world,[61] just like the demons—consists first of all in defending us against demonic attacks.[62] This they do not least in prayer as well, during which they are always present[63] in that they "dispel by [their] word alone every conflicting force [of the demons] acting in us,"[64] as we have already seen. For this reason, we must not be neglectful, for we do not want to anger those who fight for us![65]

After that, they instill in us their "irresistible" angelic thoughts,[66] which—together with our own will and the virtues deposited in our

[50]*In Ps.* 16:13 ζ.
[51]*M.c.* 19.27 ff.; *KG* III.78.
[52]*KG* VI.69.
[53]*Or.* 115.
[54]*Ibid.* 95.
[55]*KG* I.22.
[56]2 Cor 11:14; cf. *Ep.* 29.4; *Eul.* 34; *In Prov.* 20:27 (G.221).
[57]*In Prov.* 29:26 (G.370); *In Eccl.* 5:5–11 (G.38).
[58]*In Prov.* 19:4 (G.189).
[59]*Ibid.* 29:26 (G.370).
[60]*KG* VI.69.
[61]*Ibid.* III.78.
[62]*Ant. Prol.* 1.
[63]*Or.* 145.
[64]*Ibid.* 74; cf. 30.
[65]*Ibid.* 81.
[66]*Pr.* 80.

created nature like seeds—put us in a position to withstand demonic thoughts and do good.[67] In doing so, they are not always particular in their choice of educational means, for they also make use of night-time terrors and hard blows in order to bring us to the straight path.[68] The goal of this multifaceted care is always to lead us to their own angelic knowledge.

> Through the reasons of exhortation, the holy angels purify us of evil and make us impassible. Through natural and divine reasons, they free us from ignorance, making us wise men and gnostics.[69]

Accordingly, the angels impart to us the entire knowledge necessary for our salvation—consisting in *praktikē, physikē,* and *theologikē*[70]—by teaching us their own "intelligible and spiritual knowledge."[71] The "practical knowledge"[72] relating to *praktikē* deals above all with the "reasons" of the ascetic fight against the demons,[73] which allows the monk to practice "*praktikē* with knowledge."[74] The following text gives us an idea of what Evagrius understands by "the knowledge of nature."

> After frequent observation, we have found that the difference between angelic thoughts, human thoughts, and thoughts coming from the demons is as follows. First, angelic [thoughts] scrutinize the nature of things and search out their spiritual reasons. For example, why gold was created and dispersed like sand and disseminated in the valleys of the earth, and is found only with great effort and toil; and why, once found, it is washed in water and committed to the fire, and then put into the hand of artisans who fashion it into the lamps of the tabernacle and the altar of burnt offerings and the censers and the bowls,[75] from which, by the grace of our Redeemer,

---

[67]*M.c.* 31; cf. *Ep.* 18; *Sk.* 46.
[68]*KG* VI.86.
[69]*Ibid.* 35.
[70]Ibid.
[71]*Ibid.* 2; *In Ps.* 67:35 κβ.
[72]*In Ps.* 118:159 οβ.
[73]*Pr.* 83.
[74]*Ibid.* 50.
[75]Ex 25:28 ff.

the king of Babylon now no longer drinks,[76] but rather Cleopas, who bears away a heart set ablaze by such mysteries.[77]

Second, demonic thought neither understands nor knows such things. It only suggests shamelessly the acquisition of the gold that is pleasing to the senses and predicts the good life and glory that will come from this.

Lastly, human thought seeks neither to acquire gold, nor is it concerned about what gold symbolizes.[78] It merely brings before the mind the bare image of gold, devoid of the passion of greed.

By applying this rule mystically, one can say the same about other things.[79]

In a similar manner, the holy angels "illuminate" for the contemplative not only the things God has wrought, but also—as they did in the past to Daniel—"the reasons of things to come."[80] They accomplish this task until we have attained perfection in God, for then there is no longer "either pupil or teacher."[81]

The "divine reasons" (or the reasons pertaining to the divinity[82]) refer to the knowledge of God, or *theologikē*, in the narrow sense. Insofar as this knowledge is necessary for our salvation, it is contained in the "holy dogmas"[83] of the "catholic and apostolic Church"[84] and confessed in the baptismal profession of faith.[85] For this reason, it is above all the subject of faith[86] and worship,[87] and not of purely rational "exploration." Evagrius therefore also advises one to touch on these topics only rarely.[88] Our array of conceptual instruments, bor-

---

[76]Cf. Dan 5:2 f.
[77]Luke 24:18, 32.
[78]Gold in Job 28 symbolizes wisdom!
[79]*M.c.* 8.
[80]Cf. *Or.* 80.
[81]*In Ps.* 144:13 ε.
[82]Cf. *KG* I.10.
[83]*Mn.* 124.
[84]*In Prov.* 24:6 (G.266).
[85]*Mn.* 124.
[86]*Inst. mon.* (PG 79.1237D).
[87]*Gn.* 41.
[88]*In Prov.* 25:17 (G.310).

rowed from the material world, is not suitable for the knowledge of divine things.[89] Whoever does not remain constantly aware of this fact easily applies the categories developed for understanding created things to God and thus goes astray.[90] For Evagrius, true knowledge of the one God in three consubstantial hypostases—the Father, the Son, and the Holy Spirit—has an "angelic" character, unfolding in "true prayer"—the prayer "in spirit and in truth," which alone makes man a "theologian" in the proper sense![91]

**

From the example of the angels' unselfish activity, as well as their encouragement towards prayer and their own intercession for us,[92] it becomes clear that the angels are "servants of compassion and love."[93] Consequently, "resembling the angels" consists first of all in imitating the angelic virtues. Evagrius describes the activity of the "students of the angels"[94]—those aforementioned "wise men" and "gnostics," i.e. "spiritual fathers" (named thus because they "possess the gift of the Spirit and beget many for the virtue and the knowledge of God"[95])—in a way quite similar to how he describes the activity of the angels.

> Whoever has been made worthy of spiritual knowledge will help the holy angels and will lead rational souls from evil to virtue and from ignorance to knowledge.[96]

This is already the case in this present life, but will more truly be so in the "coming age," if such a man has become an "angel" properly speaking.[97] The opposite, however, is true of incompetent "patri-

---

[89]Cf. *In Eccl.* 5:1–2 (G.35).
[90]Cf. *Gn.* 41.
[91]*Or.* 60.
[92]*Ibid.* 81.
[93]Cf. *Pr.* 76.
[94]*KG* III.65.
[95]*Ep.* 52.7.
[96]*KG* VI.90; cf. V.46, 65.
[97]*Ibid.* VI.24.

archs," who on account of their long years ought to have knowledge at their disposal, but are in fact still dominated by the passions[98]:

> In the age to come,[99] an angry man will not be numbered among the angels, nor will authority[100] be entrusted to him, for he does not see because of the passions[101] and he is easily provoked against those who are led by him. He falls away from contemplation, and he endangers those [who are entrusted to him]. However, the state of angels is alien to both.[102]

Standing in utter contrast to this is the true spiritual father, who like an angel "anoint[s] us for the battles and treat[s] the wounds we suffer from the bites of wild beasts [that is, the demons]."[103] He has "heaven for [his] homeland and live[s] there constantly—not in mere word but in actions that imitate the angels and in a more God-like knowledge."[104]

> It is right to pray not only for your own purification, but also for your entire race, so as to imitate the way of the angels.[105]

In his very care for the "fallen image of God,"[106] the spiritual father (like the angels) sometimes resorts to drastic measures. On the "pure," he works like a bright "light," but on the "impure" he is like a stinging, cleansing salt.[107] Nonetheless, although he is severe with the quarrelsome,[108] he is neither threatening nor inaccessible[109] but always ready to cheer up the fainthearted.[110] Like God

---

[98]Cf. *Gn.* 31; *In Ps.* 118:100 μδ; *Mn.* 2, 112.

[99]Matt 12:32 et passim.

[100]Meant here is the authority over "five or ten cities" (Luke 19:17–19), which according to *KG* VI.24 is a symbol of knowledge.

[101]Cf. *KG* V.27.

[102]*Ibid.* IV.38 Gr.

[103]Cf. *Pr.* 100.

[104]*Or.* 142.

[105]*Ibid.* 39.

[106]*Gn.* 50.

[107]*Ibid.* 3.

[108]*Ibid.* 26.

[109]*Ibid.* 22.

[110]*Ibid.* 28.

Himself,[111] he "desires all men to be saved and to come to the knowledge of the truth."[112] His pre-eminent virtue is angelic anger-lessness.[113] Accordingly, he is prepared to suffer an injustice rather than to fight for his right.[114] In his "condescension" he is always moderate,[115] full of consideration for the spiritual maturity of his hearers.[116] Although he himself is a strict ascetic his entire life,[117] free from care about his own needs [118]and completely selfless,[119] he is always generous with alms.[120]

The main task of this angelic man is naturally teaching, and in this he is always guided by Holy Scripture correctly understood,[121] which is the revelatory source par excellence of all our knowledge.[122] Nonetheless, he always remains aware that his knowledge is inferior to that of the angels.[123] In spite of everything, he is in the end just a man, burdened with weaknesses like all men, but who in caring for others also heals himself imperceptibly.[124]

* *

As loftily as Evagrius praises the ideal of "resembling the angels," we may not forget that we are dealing here with a conceptual image. Man was neither created as an angel, nor is he destined to become "merely" an angel at the consummation of the ages! The perfect "image of God" according to which man was not only created, but also "renewed" in holy baptism, is Jesus Christ, the incarnate Son of God. The final goal in our "ascent" to God is thus not merely to be "like the

---

[111]*Ibid.* 22.
[112]I Tim 2:4.
[113]*Gn.* 5, 10, 32.
[114]*Ibid.* 8.
[115]*Ibid.* 6.
[116]*Ibid.* 13, 14, 23, 25, 35, 36.
[117]*Ibid.* 37.
[118]*Ibid.* 38.
[119]*Ibid.* 24.
[120]*Ibid.* 7.
[121]*Ibid.* 18–21, 34.
[122]*KG* VI.1; cf. II.64, 69 et passim.
[123]*Gn.* 16, 40.
[124]*Ibid.* 33.

holy powers" (ὁμοίους ταῖς ἁγίαις δυνάμεσιν), i.e. the angels, but rather to "be made like" (παρεμφέρειν) Christ!

> For the prayer of our Lord must be completely fulfilled. Indeed, it is Jesus who prays "that they may all be one; even as thou, Father, art in me, and I in thee."[125] Thus shall we be: no longer experiencing either increase or decrease in regard to knowledge, but rather living perfectly forever in the Lord.[126]

This "similarity" begins in baptism when we are "baptized into Christ and put on Christ [as a garment]"[127]: as "wisdom, righteousness, and sanctification,"[128] but also as "meekness," that quality that distinguished him from all others.[129] Consequently, we should above all "imitate" Christ here on earth[130] and become disciples of his meekness![131]

For this reason, the "bread of angels," i.e. their perfect knowledge "of the things on earth"[132] (in other words, of the ordering of creation and of the history of salvation[133]), does not ultimately suffice for man. Only Christ has perfect knowledge of the "first principle" of all things[134] in that he possesses not only the limited "contemplation of the created, but also knows him who himself created everything."[135] We must therefore eat his "bread," his "flesh" and "blood," in order to become "partakers of the Logos and the wisdom of God."[136] Naturally, the demons try to thwart this communion with all their

---

[125]John 17:21. Cf. G. Bunge, "Mysterium Unitatis: Der Gedanke der Einheit von Schöpfer und Geschöpf in der evagrianischen Mystik." *Freiburger Zeitschrift für Philosophie und Theologie* 36 (1989): 449–69.

[126]*In Ps.* 88:46 ιη.

[127]Gal 3:27.

[128]1 Cor 1:30; cf. *In Ps.* 21:19 η.

[129]*M.c.* 11.29 f.

[130]*Ibid.* 13.12 f.

[131]Cf. *Ep.* 36.3; 56.9.

[132]2 Kgs 14:20; cf. *Gn.* 16; *KG* I.23; *In Eccl.* 5:7–11 (G.38.6); *In Ps.* 4:7 ς, 29:8 ζ.

[133]*In Ps.* 118:171 ο θ et passim.

[134]*Gn.* 40.

[135]*In Ps.* 88:9 δ.

[136]*Ep. fid.* 4.15 ff.; cf. *Mn.* 118, 119.

might.[137] Only the Logos and the Spirit will one day make accessible to us the perfect knowledge of the Father.[138]

By grace, the "angel-like" man experiences this eschatological elevation of his[139] already here on earth, when purified of all passions, he is allowed to rest his head on Christ's "breast,"[140] as once did John the Evangelist and Theologian.[141] In particular, this happens "at the time of prayer" when such a man receives from the Father "the most glorious gift"[142] of true prayer "in spirit and in truth,"[143] which makes him a "theologian"[144] and thus a man who speaks not only about God and his works, but also bears witness to him from a most heartfelt intimacy. Henceforth, he no longer praises God—like the angels and the angelic man[145]—because of his creation, but in an ineffable way "he praises [God] because of himself."[146] Only the one who has experienced this himself can understand what this means.

---

[137] *In Ps.* 67:24 ιε.
[138] *Ep. Mel.* passim.
[139] *Ibid.* 54–62.
[140] *Mn.* 120; *Ep. Mel.* 67.
[141] John 13:25.
[142] *Or.* 69.
[143] *Ibid.* 58.
[144] *Ibid.* 60.
[145] *In Ps.* 118:171 οθ.
[146] *Or.* 59.

CHAPTER 12

"For His Teaching Was Very Meek"

E vagrius had a highly gifted speculative mind, and many could be tempted perhaps to dismiss his teaching on angels, men, and demons (and their virtues and vices, respectively) as mere philosophico-theological theorizing. Is he not gladly hailed as the "philosopher in the desert"? Yet by naming him thus, we overlook the fact that Evagrius, as a monk in his time, was this and more: a mystic who relied on experience, both his own and that of the fathers of his day.

Biographical and autobiographical texts attest that for Evagrius as well as his brother monks in the desert, the world of angels and demons was first a fact of experience before becoming the focus of theoretical investigation. Thus, Evagrius had experienced in his own body,[1] for example, the demonic origin of certain psychosomatic phenomena (as we would say today) and observed it in other monks[2] before he attempted to interpret these phenomena with the help of his spiritual father.[3] Likewise, the connection he makes between faith-destroying heresy and the demons[4] is not only a widespread conviction of his time, but for Evagrius also a frightening personal experience, as he emphatically attests.

> Now then, my son, listen to me now,
> and do not draw near the doors of lawless men,
> nor step into their snares, lest you be caught.
> Keep your soul far away from [their] pseudo-gnosis!

---

[1]M.c. 33; Vita H, I.
[2]Ant. VI.36, 72 etc.
[3]M.c. 33.24 ff.
[4]In Ps. 141:4 α; cf. 26:2 α.

For I too have often spoken with them,
but I spied out their words as dark,
and in them I found the venom of serpents.
In their words, there is neither sense nor wisdom.
All those who accept them perish,
and those who love them are filled with evils.
For I have seen the fathers of their teachings
and met with them in the desert—
I have encountered the enemies of the Lord,
and demons fought with me in words,
and I saw no true light in their orations.[5]

Palladius (the scholar, friend, and biographer of Evagrius) gives us a detailed account of this dramatic encounter with the demons who had sought out Evagrius in the form of clerics from heretical sects.[6]

Similar things can be said of other aspects of the spiritual life, such as the vision of the "light of the Holy Trinity"[7] about which Evagrius speaks so frequently. Evagrius owes his oft-repeated conviction that meekness is not only the "mother of knowledge," but is also of angelic origin, quite obviously to a mystical experience. Let us take note of the context of Evagrius' experience.

At another time, the spirit of blasphemy tormented him and he spent forty days without stepping under the roof of a cell, until his body became verminous, like a mindless beast.[8] A few days later, he related to us the revelations he had seen. He never concealed anything from his disciples. "It happened," he said, "that I was sitting in my cell at night, the burning lamp at my side, while I was meditating on one of the prophets. I had an ecstasy in the middle of the night, and it was as if I found myself in a dream during sleep.[9] I saw

---

[5]*Mn.* 126; cf. 123–25.
[6]*Vita* 11, also contained in the Greek text.
[7]Cf. *Ant.* VI.16.
[8]*Vita* 10.
[9]At issue here is a mystical state, which Evagrius sometimes compares with sleep (cf. *In Ps.* 126:2 γ). In such a state, one does not know that one is "in contemplation" (cf. *In Ps.* 126:2 γαλ). Since we are dealing here with a state "of complete sensation-

myself airborne, hanging from the clouds, and beheld everything with one glance. The one from whom I was hanging said: "Do you see all this?" He had in fact raised me up to the clouds and I saw the entire world at one glance. I said to him: "Yes." He said to me: "I shall give you a commandment. If you fulfill this word in deed, you will rule over all that you have seen." He then said to me: "Go, be merciful and meek, and set your thought directly on God.[10] And you will rule over all this!" When he had finished saying this to me, I saw myself again, holding the book, the wick burning, and I did not know how I had been lifted up to the clouds. "Whether in the body or out of the body I do not know, God knows."[11]

And he fought for both these virtues as though he would possess [with them] all the virtues.[12]

Evagrius must have been affected very deeply by this experience, which is not without parallel in Christian mysticism.[13] It is no accident that he alludes to Paul's rapture, an experience that likewise made a permanent mark on the apostle. At any rate, Evagrius took to heart the warning of the heavenly messenger (was it an angel, or perhaps Christ?) and made it the foundation of his ascetic-mystical teaching. Palladius continues:

He used to say that meekness leads the intellect to right knowledge in that [meekness] draws it upwards. For it is written: "He will teach the meek his ways."[14] Truly, this is the virtue of the angels . . .[15]

*

---

lessness," literally "absence of sense perception (ἀναισθησία)" (*Or.* 120), night is better for contemplation than day. Cf. *KG* V.52, to be compared with John Cassian, *Conferences* IX.31.

[10]What is likely meant here is right faith.

[11]2 Cor 12:2.

[12]*Vita* J.

[13]Cf. e.g. the famous vision of St. Benedict in: Gregory the Great, *Dial.* II.XXXV.3.

[14]Ps 24:9.

[15]*Vita* K.

Evagrius first put into practice himself what he taught others in his writings. The people who read his writings[16] or came to him in droves seeking his aid in their difficulties did this because "his teaching was very meek,"[17] as was his whole conduct.

> It was impossible to find in his mouth a worldly word or bit of sarcasm, nor did he want to hear any from others,[18]

because these sarcastic words—especially in the educated—all too often merely conceal resentment or envy. Likewise, any sign of careerism (also a manifestation of misdirected anger) was entirely foreign to him: the former deacon of the Archbishop of Constantinople even dodged his calling to be the bishop of Thmuis by fleeing to Palestine.[19] The portrait sketched in the fifth century by the church historian Sozomen (based on written or oral tradition) might thus be seen as an accurate rendering of Evagrius' character:

> It is said that his nature was modest; he subdued vanity and pride to such a degree that he was neither inflated by applause when rightly praised, nor did he become indignant at an insult when unjustly rebuked.[20]

As we know from Palladius and his personal letters, Evagrius lacked neither commendation nor censure. Even during his lifetime, his spiritual teaching aroused general interest and brought him praise, which he declined as loathsome.[21] This renown provoked many a confrère of even his immediate surroundings to harsh criticism, one example being the learnèd Heron, who declared, "One may not have another teacher than Christ"[22]—as though Evagrius had ever taught something else or had expected such from his disciples![23] Later,

---

[16]Cf. *Ep.* 4; 19.2; *Lausiac History (Syriac version) (HL syr.)* 73.4.

[17]*Vita* E.

[18]*Ibid.* L; cf. *Gn.* 32; *Eul.* 17.

[19]*Vita* G, M.

[20]Sozomen, *Ecclesiastical History* VI.30 (PG 67.1384B).

[21]*Ep.* 52.1 f.

[22]*Lausiac History (HL)* 26.1.

[23]Cf. *Vita* Ab, where a moving testimony of Palladius to his teacher is found.

Heron came to an awful fall on account of his arrogance. The case was no different for the strict ascetic Eucarpius, whom Evagrius disdainfully called the "turner of words," imputing that he led people astray with his teaching.[24] According to Evagrius' thought, both monks were victims of the demon of anger.

Moreover, Evagrius occasionally alludes in a self-deprecating way to his own undeniable cleverness with words,[25] which at one point earned him a public reprimand from his teacher: Macarius of Alexandria, a priest of the Kellia. This episode, likely known also to Sozomen, entered the *Gerontikon*, the alphabetical collection of sayings of the Fathers, which otherwise incorporated only excerpts from Evagrius' writings.

> Once there was an assembly in the Kellia on some matter and Abba Evagrius [also] spoke. The priest [Macarius] said to him: "We know, Abba, that were you in your homeland, you often could have been bishop or the leader of many. But now you live here as a foreigner." But he, filled with remorse, did not grow embarrassed; rather, he shook his head [in agreement] and said to him: "It is true, Father. However, I have spoken once; I will not do it a second time."[26]

Furthermore, Evagrius has handed down his own version of this episode and likewise its spiritual meaning, which undoubtedly hails from the early time of his residence in the Kellia. He himself may have been the anonymous brother in the following incident:

> A brother was offended by a God-fearing man. Suffering the injustice, he went away, torn back and forth between joy and grief. The first, because being treated unfairly and offended, he did not fall into bewilderment; the latter, because the God-fearing man had been mistaken and had rejoiced in his error.[27]

---

[24]*HL syr.* 73.4.
[25]*Pr.* 94.
[26]*Apophthegmata* Evagrius 7. Quotation: Job 40:5.
[27]*Eul.* 4.

Evagrius seems to mean here that Macarius had belittled him publicly, because he supposed that his disciple had spoken out of vanity, which evidently was not the case. Evagrius then continues:

> But understand that the deceiver [that is, the demon] also experienced both things, insofar as he greatly rejoiced in having confounded [the insulter], yet he was saddened all the more when [the insulted one] did not likewise fall into bewilderment.

Evagrius apparently returns later to this incident once again, declaring laconically: "If, because of your service, you journey on foreign soil, do not expect to be treated as a guest by all. Hold yourself unworthy of this honor in order to put to flight the thought of slander, even if it speaks the truth." If one is belittled, one should bless the offender, but cast his rancor on the devil,[28] since he is the author both of the insult as well as the rancor.

From this episode, which apparently hurt him deeply, Evagrius draws the conclusion that it is best that one "close the door to anger through the lips."[29] This humble silence is a sure sign of meekness, which for Evagrius became "the mother of knowledge," knowledge even of the entire demonic game of "thoughts." Even his contemporaries, especially his friend Rufinus, admired and praised his "discernment of spirits."

> There [in the Kellia as well] we saw an exceedingly wise and truly wonderful man named Evagrius, who among other good qualities of the Spirit had been granted such a gift of the "discernment of spirits"[30] and—as the Apostle says—of the "purification of thoughts"[31] that it was thought that none of the Fathers had attained such a knowledge of subtle and spiritual things.[32]

* *

---

[28] *Ibid.* 21.

[29] *Ibid.*

[30] 1 Cor 12:10.

[31] Cf. 2 Cor 10:5.

[32] *History of the Monks in Egypt* (*HM*) XXVII (7.1).

Evagrius has not left us any treatise of his own entitled *On Meekness*; yet the themes of love, meekness, and (spiritual) friendship run through his entire œuvre like a red thread. Characteristically, the most impressive texts are found in his personal letters as well as in his scholia on individual books of the Bible, which were destined for a public closely associated with the author.[33] More than in his other writings, here it becomes clear that the teaching of the monk of Pontus was really "very meek"; one has only to see how often the words "your love" are used in the letters as a form of address.[34] For the "holy"[35] and truly "divine love"[36] is, of course, God himself, according to the beloved disciple's word.[37] The "original love"[38] is that infallible sign by which one recognizes the true disciples of Christ,[39] who "is our love."[40] We see also how frequently Evagrius admonishes the addressees of his letters to be meek—that concrete manifestation of love by which one "stems anger."[41] Above all, meekness is for us a "mother of knowledge" because it turns "the intellect into a contemplative"[42]: that is, into a man whom divine grace permits to recognize things directly, "by eyesight."[43]

> Moreover, I am convinced that your meekness has turned you into a cause of great knowledge. For no other single virtue brings out wisdom so much as meekness, for whose sake Moses was also praised for being "meeker than all men." And I also pray to become and be called a disciple of "the meek one."[44]

---

[33]Cf. G. Bunge, "Der mystische Sinn der Schrift: Anläßlich der Veröffentlichung der *Scholien zum Ecclesiasten* des Evagrios Pontikos." *Studia Monastica* 36 (1994): 135–46.

[34]*Ep.* 3.4; 4.1; 12.1; 19.1; 21.2; 31.1; 35; 41.1; 58.1.

[35]*Ibid.* 60.2, 4.

[36]*Ibid.* 61.1.

[37]1 John 4:8

[38]*Ep.* 44.2; 56.3.

[39]*Ibid.* 40.3; 44.2.

[40]*Ibid.* 37.2; 40.1.

[41]*Ibid.* 19.2.

[42]*Ibid.* 27.2, 4.

[43]*Gn.* 4.

[44]*Ep.* 36.3.

Consequently, "the first and original (μία καὶ ἀρχαία) commandment is love, by which the intellect beholds the first love (τὴν πρώτην
ἀγάπην)," because God "first loved us."[45] For through our love, we
contemplate the love of God towards us, as is written in the Psalm:
"He will teach the meek his ways."[46] Yet Moses was meeker than all
men,[47] and the Holy Spirit fittingly says[48]: "He made known his ways
unto Moses."[49]

It was, on the contrary, proper to request from you the fruits of
love—you who have acquired through your impassibility divine
love[50] and have become rich with heavenly "riches."[51] "For children
ought not to lay up for their parents, but parents for their children."[52]
Therefore, since you are fathers, imitate Christ "the father"[53] and
feed us with the "barley loaf"[54] through the teaching on the
improvement of morals. Condescend to our rudeness, until we put
off our bestial customs and are made worthy of the spiritual "bread
. . . that has come down from heaven"[55] and which feeds all reason-
endowed natures according to their condition.

For "he who descended is he who also ascended far above all the
heavens, that he might fill all things."[56] And when he fulfills all
things, then "from his fullness shall we all receive."[57] For the "fullness of Christ"[58] is the spiritual knowledge of past and future worlds,
together with true faith in the Holy Trinity.

---

[45]1 John 4:19.
[46]Ps 24:9.
[47]Num 12:3.
[48]Ps 102:7.
[49]Ep. 56.3, both Gr. and Syr.
[50]Cf. Pr. 81.
[51]Meant here is wisdom; cf. Wis 7:14; also Ep. 47, note 1.
[52]2 Cor 12:14.
[53]On Christ as "father," cf. In Prov. 20:9 (G.210).
[54]John 6:9. This "barley loaf" symbolizes here praktikē.
[55]John 6:38, 42, 51. The "spiritual bread" is a symbol of heavenly knowledge.
[56]Eph 4:10.
[57]John 1:16.
[58]Eph 3:19; 4:13.

But perfect faith is acquired by renouncing all thoughts of bodily things. And the Holy Trinity reveals itself to the intellect [so that the intellect may contemplate it][59] when it has freed itself of passions and the "old man . . . who is corrupt through deceitful lusts."[60] But when the latter is destroyed, it becomes a total sacrifice to God through an upright mode of life and true faith.[61]

---

[59]The sentence in brackets is missing from some manuscripts.
[60]Eph 4:22.
[61]*Ep.* 61.

Epilogue

We have arrived at the end of our journey through Evagrius' writings. The effort will have been worthwhile if it has set the reader to thinking. Much will have already been gained if his aggressiveness appears to him less "natural" than it has up to now, especially if he has become aware that its consequences (as Evagrius understands them) are even entirely unnatural—that is, they are diametrically opposed to his original created destiny. With this understanding, he will not yet have come to grips with the irrational power of irascibility, but a goal has come into sight: a human image of great value and inner unity. For it is not a matter of the suppression of our natural powers, not even of the irrational ones, but rather of their purification and unification. Only a soul that is entirely united in its three "parts" becomes unassailable for the demons that will plague us until death. To be a Christian means to fight.

> Just as an athlete cannot be crowned
> if he does not contend in the wrestling match,
> so too can no one become a Christian
> without a struggle.[1]

Indeed, our life resembles a battlefield on which the demons, through their seductive "thoughts," fight against us most fiercely in order to bring about this unnatural operation of the powers of the soul, which we call "vice." However, we do not stand alone in this battle. We have the example and teaching of Christ, who indeed has already vanquished Satan, as well as the powerful help of God's angels. If man is defeated in the fight, this is not due to the superior strength of the enemies, and even less to the negligence of the helpers,

---

[1]*Inst. mon.* (PG 79.1236B).

but only to our lukewarmness![2] We are, of course, entirely free to consent to the "demonic thoughts" of our opponents or the "angelic thoughts" of our helpers, and then to lead the life of a demon or an angel. If man imitates the predominant characteristic of a demon (anger), he himself becomes a "demon" and "serpent." On the contrary, if he makes "the angelic manner" his own by imitating the "virtue of the angels" (meekness), he acquires an "almost angelic state," even becoming "like an angel." Both have far-reaching consequences! If anger "blinds" him, meekness turns him into a "contemplative," i.e. a "beholder" of the mysteries of God and his creation.

*

Anger and meekness, then, are antagonists. They represent two fundamental and mutually exclusive attitudes. As little as meekness is mere weakness—the "meek one" ought to be "a fighter"—so little does this gentleness combine with aggressiveness in the modern sense of the word. That seems obvious, even self-evident; and yet experience teaches that many people try to combine these two basic attitudes. More precisely, in word they hold to the Christian ideal of love, but their presumed "holy zeal" for the truth, in which, according to Evagrius, one must "persevere, even when one is therefore shown enmity,"[3] has all too frequently as its hidden motive not this love, but anger. This becomes clear when their irascibility is directed not only against the demons and the evil caused by them (among which heresy is included), but also turns against sinners and heretics: "but anger is completely unjustified against your neighbor."[4]

The basic error of these zealots, who have already caused so much harm in the Church, is of course of a spiritual nature. Evagrius strongly warns against this:

> Approve of no abstention that banishes meekness![5]

---

[2]*Ant. Prol.* 1, 2.
[3]*Gn.* 44.
[4]Cf. *Or.* 24.
[5]*Ep.* 56.5 Gr.

Moderation or "self-mastery" (ἐγκράτεια) is a bridle for desire, just as meek love heals anger from unnatural impulses. However, both are authentic only when they are present together in the soul.[6] Abstention, asceticism without love, is not virtue but vice. The demons, of course, need neither sleep nor food and such things.[7] Whoever does not understand this had better not first set foot on the monastic path. Evagrius, who champions such a high and angelic ideal of monasticism, is also the severest judge of his sodality:

> Better a meek, worldly man
> than an angry, raving monk[8];
> Better a sweet-tempered wife
> than a raving, angry virgin.[9]

Such a false "Nazirite" who secretly becomes enraptured with the forbidden "dragon's wine" of anger is a deceiver, leading people astray by his "holy garment,"[10] which symbolizes[11] in all its parts those virtues he does not possess. Such deceit is not without danger.

> Whoever causes offence to worldly people
> will not remain unpunished,
> and whoever embitters them
> disgraces his Name,[12]

that beautiful name of "Christ," which of course is derived from what he has said about himself: "Learn from me, for I am meek and lowly in heart."

*

According to the testimony of his friends, Palladius and Rufinus, Evagrius himself was an extremely austere ascetic,[13] "of incredible

---

[6] *Pr.* 35, 38.
[7] Macarius the Egyptian 11.
[8] *Mn.* 34, cf. 78.
[9] *Vg.* 45.
[10] *Pr.* Prologue (9).
[11] *Ibid.* (1–7).
[12] *Mn.* 113.
[13] *Vita* B, C, D.

abstinence."[14] Not only was his "teaching very meek," his entire "nature also was very unassuming." Accordingly, the following excerpt from one of his personal letters reads like a spiritual testament, behind which stands the entire weight of an upright life.

> As for myself, I am one of those who praise abstinence, and I therefore pray to live with you, together with forbearance and love. For without these, what should one call abstinence? It is ashes left behind by the fire, which the incandescence of love has burned, for abstinence alone resembles that foolish virgin who was excluded from the bridal chamber when her oil ran out and her lamp was extinguished.[15] I call the intellect a "lamp," which was created to receive the blessed "light"[16] and which, because of its hardening, has fallen away from the knowledge of God. Wherever "oil" is lacking,[17] there anger rules. I had to tell you this, my dear brother.[18]

How different the history of the Church would look—the Church, which of course is the foundation of "meekness"—if its members, shepherds, and flock had taken this "meek teaching" more sincerely to heart, especially when dealing with truth and "right belief."

> Anger squanders knowledge,
> forbearance gathers it in.[19]

Let us not be deceived: anger "blinds" not only the one who has objectively deviated from the truth and has become a "heretic," but also the one to whom the truth was entrusted and who seeks to defend it. How can there be "true knowledge" where, full of anger and resentment, one opposes real or supposed "heresies," i.e. where this has not been admitted? Most often, this involves a fellow Christian suspected of heresy. A man may be quite the great faster and ascetic,

---

[14]*HM* XXVII (7.3).
[15]Matt 25:1 ff.
[16]"Light" here symbolizes knowledge; cf. *Ep.* 28, note 3.
[17]A symbol of "holy love"; cf. *KG* IV.25 and *Ep.* 28, note 4.
[18]*Ep.* 28.1.
[19]*Mn.* 35.

yet all this abstinence is of no avail if instead he is overwhelmed by other passions: namely, resentment, anger, vainglory, and arrogance.

> Be not uncritical, I beg you, and do not think that only those who fast receive the knowledge of God! No ship is finished with one board, nor is a house built with one brick.[20]

When "the world is in uproar," the wise man stays away from all "destructive discussions."[21] For what else do they produce but those "divisions of the Church of the Lord," which are nothing else but the bitter fruits of anger? Here the judgment of Evagrius is of prophetic severity:

> Whoever plunges the Lord's Church into confusion,
> him will the fire consume,
> and whoever resists the priest,
> him will the earth devour,[22]

just like Korah and his party, who rebelled against Moses and Aaron.[23] The Lord does not accept the "incense" of these angry rebels because their prayer offends him.[24] Here too Evagrius speaks once again categorically:

> Those who divide the Lord's Church are far removed from pure prayer![25]

Prayer that is "pure" from all passions, above all from anger, is an exceedingly noble good. The demons leave no stone unturned in their attempts to "disturb" it. To this aim, they overwhelm in particular those who have already advanced quite far in the spiritual life with all sorts of defamation in order to provoke them to anger.[26]

> The demons never cease to defame the gnostic, even when he has not made a mistake, in order to attract his intellect to themselves. A

---

[20] *Ep.* 52.6.
[21] *Ibid.* 52.5.
[22] *Mn* 114. "Priest" (πρεσβύτερος) here refers to the bishop.
[23] Cf. Num 16:1 ff.
[24] Cf. *O. Sp.* 4.18.
[25] *Ep.* 52.5.
[26] Cf. *Gn.* 32.

cloud unfolds around the intellect and leads it away from contemplation to the time when it finds the demons guilty as slanderers.[27]

If the "slanderers" already bring this to pass with some success
among the innocent, "what will they then do when they find such a
pretext" as the "dividing of the Lord's Church"?![28]

Finally, what should one think of this unwillingness to forgive,
another form of resentment, the "remembrance of evil" [real or imagined to have been suffered],[29] which makes every reconciliation
impossible? In the same letter in which he writes that "no other evil
turns the intellect into a demon as anger," Evagrius strongly urges:

> Teach your brothers the meekness [of Moses], and be not slow to
> accept repentance for anger.[30]

To restore the "unanimity of the Church," both are needed—
meekness and steadfastness—as Evagrius writes, probably to John II,
Bishop of Jerusalem[31]: meekness towards the erring and steadfastness
against error.

Might this "very meek teaching" of Evagrius, who in no wise
lacked inner strength, be able to point out even to modern-day Christians the way back to this "consonance of rational souls who say the
same thing and among whom there are no schisms"[32]—a road from
which they have strayed now for so long? For this "consonance" (συμ-
φωνία), as in a polyphonic "choir," is no humanly understandable
utopian vision. On the contrary, it is a divine gift, which Christ
besought and obtained from the Father for us[33] and which one can
only safeguard in humility by "abiding" in it[34]—or, as the case may be,
by returning to it in true repentance[35] when it has been lost.

---

[27] KG III.90 Gr.
[28] Ep. 52.5.
[29] Pr. 11.
[30] Ep. 56.4 Gr.
[31] Ibid. 24.2.
[32] In Ps. 150:4 α, ε.
[33] John 17.
[34] John 15.
[35] Rev 2:5.

Bibliography

Ant

    Antirrhetikos, ed. W. Frankenberg, in *Evagrius Ponticus, Abhandlungen der königlichen Gesellschaft der Wissenschaften zu Göttingen*, Philologisch-historische Klasse, Neue Folge 13.2 (Berlin: Weidmannsche Buchhandlung, 1912).

Ant Prol

    Prolog des Antirrhetikos, cf. G. Bunge, *Evagrios Pontikos: der Prolog des Antirrhetikos*. Studia Monastica 39.1 (1997): 77–105.

Ep

    Epistulae I–LXII, ed. W. Frankenberg, trans. by G. Bunge in: *Briefe aus der Wüste. Sophia* 24 (Trier: Paulinus-Verlag, 1986). Greek fragments: C. Guillaumont, "Fragments grecs inédits d'Évagre le Pontique," in: *Texte und Textkritik*, ed. J. Dummer, 209–21. *Texte und Untersuchungen* 133 (Berlin: Akademie-Verlag, 1987). P. Géhin. "Nouveaux fragments grecs des lettres d'Évagre." *Revue d'histoire des textes* 24 (1994): 117–47.

Ep. fid.

    Epistula fidei, ed. J. Gribomont, in: M. Forlin-Patrucco, *Basilio di Cesarea, Le lettere*. Vol. I (Corona Patrum 11) (Turin: Società editrice internazionale, 1983), 84–113. German translation in G. Bunge, *Briefe aus der Wüste* (see above).

Ep. Mel.

    Epistula ad Melaniam, ed. W. Frankenberg; G. Vitestam, *Seconde partie du traité qui passe sous le nom de "La grande lettre d'Évagre le Pontique à Mélanie l'Ancienne."* Scripta minora regiae societatis humaniorum litterarum Lundensis 1963–1964. Vol. 3. (Lund: Glerrup, 1964). German translation in G. Bunge, *Briefe aus der Wüste* (see above).

Eul

Tractatus ad Eulogium monachum. Short recension found in: J. Migne (ed.) *Patrologia graeca* (PG 79.1093–1140A). English version consulted for this translation in: Robert E. Sinkewicz (trans.), *Evagrius of Pontus. The Greek Ascetic Corpus* (*Oxford Early Christian Studies*) (Oxford: Oxford University Press, 2003).

Gn

Gnostikos, ed. A. and C. Guillaumont, *Évagre le Pontique. Le gnostique, ou, À celui qui est devenu digne de la science: Édition critique des fragments grecs; Traduction intégrale établie au moyen des versions syriaques et arménienne; Commentaire et tables. Sources Chrétiennes* (SC) 356 (Paris: Éditions du Cerf, 1989).

In Eccl

Scholia in Ecclesiasten, ed. P. Géhin, *Évagre le Pontique, Scholies à l'Ecclésiaste.* SC 397 (Paris: Éditions du Cerf, 1993).

In Prov

Scholia in Proverbia, ed. P. Géhin, *Évagre le Pontique, Scholies aux Proverbes.* SC 340 (Paris: Éditions du Cerf, 1987).

InPs

Scholia in Psalmos. With kind permission from M.-J. Rondeau, who is preparing an edition of this work. We are using the collation made by her of the Ms *Vaticanus graecus* 754. Cf. also: "Le commentaire sur les Psaumes d'Évagre le Pontique." *Orientalia Christiana Periodica* (OCP) 26 (1960): 307–48.

Inst. Mon.

Institutio ad Monachos, PG 79.1236–1240. Supplement: ed. J. Muyldermans, "Evagriana. Le Vatic. Barb. Graec. 515." *Le Muséon. Revue d'Études Orientales* 51 (1938): 191–226, esp. 198 ff.

KG

Kephalaia Gnostika, ed. A. Guillaumont. *Les six Centuries des "Kephalaia Gnostica" d'Évagre le Pontique, Patrologia Orientalis* 28.1 (Paris: Firmin-Didot, 1958).

M.c.

De diversis malignis cogitationibus, ed. P. Géhin, C. Guillaumont, A. Guillaumont, *Évagre le Pontique. Sur les pensées.* SC 438 (Paris: Éditions du Cerf, 1998).

Mn

Sententiae ad monachos, ed. H. Gressmann, *Nonnenspiegel und Mönchsspiegel des Evagrios Pontikos. Texte und Untersuchungen* 39.4 (Leipzig: Hinrichs, 1913), 143–65.

Or

De oratione tractatus, PG 79.1165–1200. Corrected by Ms. *Coislin* 109 (Paris: Bibliothèque nationale) and the *Philokalia*, 1:176 ff. (Athens: Astēr, 1957).

O.Sp.

Tractatus de octo spiritibus malitiae, PG 79.1145–1164. Transl. by G. Bunge, *Evagrios Pontikos. Über die acht Gedanken* (Würzburg: Echter-Verlag, 1992). Also known in one recension as *On the Eight Thoughts.* English version consulted for this translation in: Robert E. Sinkewicz (trans.), *Evagrius of Pontus. The Greek Ascetic Corpus* (*Oxford Early Christian Studies*) (Oxford: Oxford University Press, 2003).

Pr

Praktikos (*Capita practica ad Anatolium*), ed. A. and C. Guillaumont, *Évagre le Pontique. Traité pratique ou le moine,* SC 170/171 (Paris: Éditions du Cerf, 1971). German trans. by G. Bunge, *Evagrios Pontikos. Praktikos, oder, der Mönch: Hundert Kapitel über das geistliche Leben. Schriftenreihe des Zentrums patristischer Spiritualität Koinonia-Oriens im Erzbistum Köln* 32 (Cologne: Luther-Verlag, 1989). [English translations consulted: John Eudes Bamberger (trans.), *Evagrius Ponticus. The Praktikos. The Chapters on Prayer.* Cistercian Studies Series, Number Four (Kalamazoo, MI: Cistercian Publications, 1970); and Robert E. Sinkewicz (trans.), *Evagrius of Pontus. The Greek Ascetic Corpus* (*Oxford Early Christian Studies*) (Oxford: Oxford University Press, 2003).]

Sent.

Sexti Pythagorici, Clitarchi, Evagrii Pontici Sententiae, ed. A. Elter, *Gnomica. Vol. 1: Sexti Pythagrici, Clitarchi, Evagrii Pontici Sententiae* (Leipzig: BG Teubner, 1892).

Sk

Skemmata, ed. J. Muyldermans, *"Evagriana." Le Muséon. Revue d'Études Orientales* 44 (1931): 37–68. Revised and reprinted as: *Evagriana. Extrait de la revue Le Muséon* 44, *augmenté de: Nouveaux fragments grecs inédits* (Paris: Paul Geuthner, 1931).

Vg

Sententiae ad virginem, ed. H. Gressmann, *Nonnenspiegel und Mönchsspiegel des Euagrios Pontikos. Texte und Untersuchungen* 39.4 (Leipzig: Hinrichs, 1913), 143–65.

Vit

De vitiis quae opposita sunt virtutibus, PG 79.1140 ff.

Additional Source Texts

Conf

Conferences (Conlationes), John Cassian. Ed. M. Petschenig, in: E. Pichéry, *Jean Cassien, Conférences*, SC 42/54 (Paris: Éditions du Cerf, 1955/1958/1959). [English version: C. Luibheid (trans.), *John Cassian, Conferences* (Classics of Western Spirituality series) (Mahwah, NJ: Paulist Press, 1985)].

HL

Historia Lausiaca, Palladius. Ed. C. Butler (Cambridge, 1898 and 1904). [English version: R.T. Meyer (trans.), *Palladius. The Lausiac History* (Ancient Christian Writers series No. 34) (Mahwah, NJ: Paulist Press, 1965).]

HM

Historia Monachorum in Aegypto, Rufinus. E. Schultz-Flügel (ed.), *Tyrannius Rufinus. Historia Monachorum in Aegypto sive de Vita Sanctorum Patrum (Patristische Texte und Studien)* (Berlin: Walter de Gruyter, 1990). [English version: F.X. Murphy (transl.), *Rufinus of Aquileia* (Washington, DC: Catholic University Press, 1945)].

HL syr.

R. Draguet, ed., *Les formes syriaques de la matière de l'Histoire Lausiaque*. *Corpus Scriptorum Christianorum Orientalium* (CSCO) 389/390 and 398/399 (Louvain/Leuven: Peeters, 1979).

Vita

Vita Evagrii coptice, Palladius. Cf. G. Bunge and A. de Vogüé, *Quatre ermites égyptiens, d'après les fragments coptes de l'"Histoire Lausiaque." Spiritualité Orientale* (SO) 60 (Bégrolles-en-Mauges [Maine-et-Loire]: Abbaye de Bellefontaine, 1994), 153–75.

General Index

Definition and core pages are indicated by boldface numbers.

Rufinus 128, 135

Sadness 33, 38, 40, 55, 63–64
Sanctification 121
Satan(ic) 9, 10, 28–29, 31, 33, 47, 64, 133
Senses 17, 25, 79; five s. of the body, 67;
five spiritual s. of the intellect, 67
Shimei the Benjaminite 86
Sinner 13, 44, 88
Slander 19, 37, 85–87
Solomon 38, 84
Song of Songs 68
Soul, the three parts (or powers) of 15,
16, 20–21, 35, 37, 43, 110; governing
power (*hēgēmonikon*) of, 16, 80; irascible power (*thymikon*) of, 11, 15–17,
20, 24, 26, 35, 37, 39, 43–44, 45–46, 51,
52, 56, 76, 78, 90, 95; concupiscible or
desiring power (*epithymētikon*) of, 15,
35, 43, 52, 76, 94; passionate part of,
16, 20–21; rational part (*logistikon*)
of, 15, 19, 21, 35, 37, 43, 52; irrational
part(s) [or power(s)] of, 11, 15, 16, 18,
21, 35, 37, 51, 60; vineyard of the s., 47;
unified and pacified s., 17; the noetic
eye of the s., 87; the soul's left eye, 68,
73, 105; the right eye, 68, 105
Sozomen 126–127
Spiritual, blindness 68; s. father(s), 65,
114, 118, 119, 120, 123; s. love, 12, 19, 45,
79, 81, 84, 100; s. seal, 112; s. altar, 81;
s. life, 23, 81; s. knowledge, 130; s.
teaching, 89; s. teacher, 99; s. children 114; s. master 70; s. reasons, 99

Stumbling Block 29, 63, 85
Suspicion(s) 40, 107

Tears before God 42, 66
Tekoa 111
Temptation(s) 17, 31, 39, 41, 48, 61, 71, 82
Thoughts, eight evil generic, 23, 35, 37,
38; angelic t. , 115–116, 134; demonic
t., 39, 44–45, 60, 62, 68, 73, 88, 116,
133–134; bestial t., 22
Trees of Paradise 29, 33

Vainglory 23, 37, 84, 87–88, 137
Vanity 19, 128
Vice(s) 10, 11, 23, 24–26, 30, 31, 34, 35, 37,
38, 41–42, 43, 47, 59, 72–73, 75, 78, 109,
110, 133; of the body, 37; of the soul,
37
Virtue(s) 11, 12, 25, 35, 43, 45, 48, 55, 69,
70, 72, 75, 77, 83, 102, 103, 109, 111, 115,
120; v. the of the angels, 118, 134;
seeds of v., 25; wisdom, the first of all
the v., 20
Visual concepts (*theōrhēmata*) 70

Wisdom 121, 130
Withdrawal (*anachōrēsis*) 55, 56; external, 55; internal, 55
Wrath (*orgē*) 10, 39, 40, 45–47, 51–53, 56,
60, 67, 69, 79, 84, 88, 109; blind, 67

Zebedee 29
Zechariah 31
Zosimas, Abba 87